Threads

Threads

2011

Editors

Jaime Barrett

Noah Kucij

Ethan Roy

Sara Tedesco

BEDFORD/ST. MARTIN'S

Boston ♦ New York

Threads is a journal of student writing and art published by the English, Modern Languages, and ESL Department at Hudson Valley Community College, Troy, New York.

Special Thanks
Maria Palmara, Department Chair
The Graphics Department
The Print Shop

Manufactured in the United States of America.

6 5 4 3 2 1
f e d c b a

For information, write: Bedford/St. Martin's, 75 Arlington Street, Boston, MA 02116 (617-399-4000)

ISBN-13: 978-1-4576-0645-8

Cover art: "Venus Eye Snap," by Vicki Bower

Message from the Editors

We would like to thank all the students who submitted their work to *Threads* this year. We received many quality submissions, and we continue to read with pleasure the enthusiasm and creativity each submission presents. Of course, all pieces have merit, and we would like to publish everything submitted, but the limitations of space will simply not allow it.

It is important to note that *Threads* reflects works that are not necessarily perfect in their format and composition, but exhibit insight, creativity, social awareness, and a unique perspective. These works—of poetry, fiction, nonfiction, and visual art— reflect the range of experience, culture, and imagination of the Hudson Valley Community College student. The editors relish the opportunity to travel and explore the territory each new issue stakes out.

Every year we are extremely pleased to highlight the exceptional work of the students at Hudson Valley Community College. Please plan your submission for next year.

Please submit your work to *Threads* electronically. Visit us at **threads.hvcc.edu**, or e-mail your work to **threads@hvcc.edu**.

Jaime Barrett
Noah Kucij
Ethan Roy
Sara Tedesco

Contents

Threads

Poetic Junkie

Elizabeth Haynes

I am a poetic junkie.
I'm addicted to truth.
My hands twitch to write down my confessions,
Write down my reactions to your ignorance,
And I love it.
I let the ink replace the blood that runs in my veins,
Take me out of the darkness,
Break down my walls.
I can't hide from myself and I love it.
This drug gives me visions,
Visions of my grandmother dancing with her angels because she
has no reason to cry,
No reason to dwell in her past because she is in a better place;
Visions of my father begging for mercy from his demons,
Trying to break the chains of his insecurities;
Visions of my mother loving her enemies with a broken heart,
Smiling through her tears.
I'm blind.
I can't see the lies you try to make me believe.
All I can see is the tears you try to hide,
The blood on the streets,
Your insecurities,
The rage in your eyes.
All I can see is truth.
I'm addicted.
The drug forces me to keep it real.
It heals me from my pain.

It helps me enjoy the rain.
I don't have the energy to fight,
All I want to do is love.
I am a poetic junkie,
And no, it's not a problem.

Therapy

Chance Hazelnis

"I got a cross tattooed on my left arm because at the time it wasn't right, I got my dad on my right arm because he left, but on the inside he was right for doing it."It's a fact that most people interpret this statement as an explanation as to why I got the tattoos that I have; however, it's actually a glimpse into how I coped with some of the scariest, most frustrating, and most joyous times in my life. I see my tattoos as not only a reflection of myself and my experiences, but also as a brief glimpse into the on-going therapy session of my life.

I was eighteen years old and it was a week prior to my high school graduation when I was very fortunate to have experienced my first "therapy session," an experience that undoubtedly changed my life. Looking back, I now know I got the cross because I needed to be able to have something with me at all times that I could revert to for strength, but I got it on my left arm due to the fact that, at the time, my religion was not making sense; so, since it wasn't right to me at the time, I got it on my left arm. This first tattoo was done at a point in time where I was getting into a lot of trouble, hanging out with the wrong crowd, and creating a lot of disappointment amongst my family. These were the things I spoke about with the my tattoo artist Rodger while getting this first tattoo, and our conversation, from time to time, still echoes in my head to this day. Rodger said to me, "You see kid, people get a tattoo for one of three reasons: (1) they want to remember, (2) they want to honor a memory of someone or something, or (3) they just want to try and be cool. Now all of those reasons except one are about remembering." Rodger then went on to explain that there is one exception to the rule, which is getting a tattoo to help deal with pain. It was at that moment when I looked down at my arm to see the needle ripping through my flesh creating a few faint blood drops every couple of centimeters that I realized that for first time in a while I wasn't in pain or in fear. I actually felt the pain and fear kind of slowly dissolving away as the tattoo went on, and after I was done and I was leaving the shop, Rodger asked me, "So kid, did your first therapy session help any?"

In anticipation of returning to Florida from my vacation in New York in a few days, I found myself at my last stop and at one of my favorite hangouts as a kid, which was the home of the Harris family. I sat on their front porch with my buddy John and his father Paul, a man that through the years had been my coach, my friend, my mentor, and pretty much more of a father to me than my own. We sat around catching up on the time I had spent living in Florida and I found myself taking in the peace and serenity of the whole situation when I was abruptly interrupted by a phone call from my mother. Upon my answer, my mother asked to speak with Paul, and after just mere moments on the phone and a look of shear panic on Paul's face, I knew something was terribly wrong. Paul then proceeded to tell me that I had to go straight home as soon as possible. Upon returning home, I found my mother crying in the kitchen, at which point she told me that my father had been found dead. I found myself at a complete and total loss for words, and as everything seemed to go into slow motion, I began to lower myself to the chair before me at the table. I can remember sitting there with my hand over my mouth in complete and utter disbelief rubbing my cross on my left arm, I guess in attempt to muster up some strength, but shockingly I wasn't surprised that this man had passed away because he had already been long since dead to me.

It was a few days later when I found myself again going under the needle, but this time with a new "therapist" named John

C. Kelsey. I remember sitting in the chair ever so impatient to get the thing started when my hands started to sweat. I started to become very nervous when I spotted the shiny, almost glistening, metallic reflection of the tattoo needle as he locked it into place on the tattoo gun. I was mesmerized by the buzzing of the tattoo gun sucking up ink like a cobra swaying to the music from a snake charmer. Unlike my first tattoo I felt that pain on every stroke of the needle for this one, but it wasn't until I saw my blood creating almost a highlight for the black letters that read, "The time was & is now," that I even noticed that pain. It was at this point I completely lost it, entering a state of total hysteria. Alarmed at my crying John stopped to which I yelled, "Unless I'm unable to sit still keep going!!"The realization that my father was gone had finally sunk in. I knew wholeheartedly that now I would never be able to fix our relationship, that I would never be able to explain to him how him not being there affected me, that I would never be able to hear in his words why he did what he did, and there wasn't a damn thing I could do to stop this pain from exposing itself; I didn't even know why it was all coming out then. What I do know is that the physical pain from the tattoo jump-started my grieving process, and in turn helped me to begin to come to terms with my loss.

Though the reasoning behind getting each of my tattoos may vary from piece to piece, they all ultimately are characterized by my desire for remembrance. I never want to be at a point where I forget what I've gone through and emotions encountered during that process because they are what has helped to make me into the person I've become today.

In the Valley

Marilyn Jarosz

I stand in the Valley on a cold damp day. I see, I hear, I feel beneath the gray and lifeless sky that stretches in all directions before me.

Buildings of cement now stand strong and protective around me, and with eyes of glass, they reveal a transparent heart encased beneath their stony armor. Revealed in them is the hope of knowledge and learning offered within their walls, and to take hold of their promise to succeed, one must merely enter with a willing mind.

These monuments to knowledge now stand huddled in the midst of brown and barren trees whose branches reach heavenward, as the rain and snow tauntingly remind them of their wintry plight. Each stronghold also stands nestled from behind by tall green pines that struggle to compensate for the Valley's winter with the promise of life and hope resting gently on their emerald branches. If only the trees could tell the story of all they've seen unfolding here over the years, as so many scholars came and went and academia grew greater in the Valley.

At the center of it all, a flag—our flag—bows her dampened head with helplessness, waiting patiently for the sun to share its warmth and the wind to wipe dry her tears. How long until the rains retreat and her great stripes unfurl with pride again in the heart of the Valley? As she now falls listless against the dismal sky, I whisper a prayer of thanks for all those who have sacrificed for freedom, so that my flag and I could both continue to stand in the Valley.

Neither rain nor snow can deter the sojourners now as they follow the paths laid out before them. Though the slush beneath their feet causes them to take each step with caution, it does not hinder them as they continue on their arduous journey. In spite of their struggle, they move forward with their eyes fixed solely upon their final destination across the Valley floor. With a determined spirit, they persevere through the Valley and find shelter as they enter the halls of promise.

I stand in the Valley now, reflecting on life, and pause to consider the struggles that have surrounded me at times. I remain steadfast and hopeful as I continue on my own journey, embracing my future with a sense of passion and purpose. I am encircled by anchors of strength, as I now stand gazing across the Valley floor with my own vision set firmly in place. I, too, have taken hold of the promises whispered here, while also seeking wisdom to guide me toward my journey's end.

Though my time here may be brief, I, too, have become a part of the Valley. I am a page in its history, existing for a moment in its present, as my own future unfolds in its tomorrow.

My Place

Robert Danzy Jr.

Where do you work and what kind of impact does your job or business have on you? As for me, I previously owned a pawn shop in Albany. In this frenzied business there is someone always trying to sell you something. In order to make money, you have to work quickly and efficiently, because the environment is very fast paced. You need a few employees to maintain the flow of traffic coming into your business. You have to log down every transaction for each customer you do business with; this in itself takes up a big part of the day. I employed someone just to fill out the paperwork that goes to the police department twice a week. Here, I will attempt to vividly explain some things I go through on a daily basis.

As I think about the sounds of business, redundancy comes to mind. If you sit back and listen, you will hear the tapping of a keyboard or the clicking of a mouse throughout almost every point of the day. There is always someone bringing something in to sell, so you're constantly on the computer looking up a price. You have to work quickly due to the amount of customers waiting to be seen. There is rarely a time when you can sit around. When I would get a second, I would take the time to do something constructive. This brings me to a humming sound that would fill the room. It was me vacuuming the floor with a track-star–like trot to beat the next rush of customers coming into the store. Another sound I can recall would be an annoyed grunt, or a disgusted moan, because the owner of an item was not happy with a price given. In this business, which is to make a profit, the customer is usually not happy with the 25 percent price we offer him or her. The customer does not understand that we cannot sell the product for what it sells for in the store. Hence, the price we offer is more than fair.

The distinct smells of my store were very powerful. The sprinkle of Carpet Fresh and misty sprays of Lysol give the store a countryside smell. You want to create a warm and comfortable environment for customers, even though they are in the store for a short period of time. You never know who might walk into your business, so you need to be prepared for whoever walks through the door. Occasionally, a skunkish aroma would tickle my nostrils from the local drunk or crackhead entering the store. Due to the rampant rush of customers, the terrible stench would linger around the store for most of the day. Some days I would be so tied up that I would not notice the smell until another customer brought it to my attention.

The last topic I will like to write on would be the utter despair of some customers at times. You feel sorry for someone who has to sell their wedding ring or something really close to their heart. In this business, you hear tons of sob stories, which most of the time are made up because the customer feels they will help to get more money. This is a business where your skin has to be extremely thick, but at the same time you have to know when someone is sincerely in need. Due to the excruciating pace of the business, you cannot waste much time talking to customers about their problems. The time you spend doing that would take away from someone else who has a transaction.

In conclusion, I want to reiterate that my store was very hectic. Some days lunch breaks were out of the question for staff. I remember eating my lunch while helping a customer because I was feeling faint. This business can be very lucrative but at the same time very stressful. You have to decide if the money is worth the stress and the constant activity that comes with owning a pawn shop.

Anybody's Daughter

Rochel Rubin

Before I could even open my eyes,
My nutrition came from fat supplies.
My mama's warm tissue I clutched
And worked my mouth as I sucked.

When I was a toddler and oh so young,
I followed my mama's behind as she sung
Around the house we puttered together
Cleaning, tidying, making the house better.

When I was five, I went part day
To be with other kids, learn, play.
But one doll stood out—not one I'd seen—
Her waist so thin, and arms so lean.

I played with Cabbage Patch Kids and Teletubbies
But my friends made fun, and said they were "Chubbies!"
Confused, I went home, ate lunch, and saw
My mama's figure, which I adored.

But as time went on and I played some more,
My mama's figure, I'd learned, was an eyesore.
I began to skip breakfast, feeding the dog,
And watched what I ate, kept a log.

For a short while I lost weight, no one could see,
Now I was happy—I was like Barbie.

The dizziness and self-chiding were worth the trouble,
Until I could no longer focus and began seeing double.

My mama in her strong arms, took me to the doc,
He said, "Something's not right, her body's in shock."
So I stayed home for weeks, which was hard for me,
But I felt my mama's figure and her warmth encompassed me.

Time heals all wounds, they say, but this seemed never ending,
Until I began to eat properly and quit all my pretending.
Now my waist is real and so are my goals and vision for
the future.
I look forward to being a "Big Mama" with a baby to nurture.

Crown of Thorns

Robert Clyde Anderson

That was the Easter of sixth grade. Dressing for church, I ducked into my parents' bathroom to check my new outfit in the big plate glass mirror: a gold turtleneck and coordinating jacket in a boxy plaid. My mom was just finishing up, fussing awkwardly with a chiffon scarf she'd draped around her collar and fastened with a glittery brooch.

"What ya think?" she asked, "Does this look ok?"

"Ughh! You're just trying to look like Mrs. Gilchrist," I groaned.

She yanked the scarf away, ripping it, tore off the pin, and slammed it into the drawer. As she hurried out of the room, I saw that her eyes were wet.

Mrs. Gilchrist was my mother's best friend. Her daughter, Debbie, was two years ahead of me in school, and our families attended the same small town Methodist Church. Now Roberta Gilchrist was a bitch of the first order, but I thought she was the most glamorous woman I'd ever known. I eavesdropped on conversations where Roberta and my mom sucked down Virginia Slims at the avocado green Formica table in Roberta's perfectly appointed Sears kitchen. She spoke condescendingly to my mom about her husband the successful football coach, her perfect daughter, her new garbage disposal. I listened, fascinated, while she talked about her years abroad as the wife of an army staff sergeant, about how she'd seen Paris and Berlin and Munich, and about how she'd actually flown in a plane to get there.

Her fashion sense was miles beyond my mother's. Roberta hit a stylistic note somewhere between Fredrick's of Hollywood and Lady Byrd Johnson. She had a good figure and often wore simple tight-fitting sheaths, accessorized with a contrasting scarf fastened by a shoulder pin. Her breasts were showcased in some kind of foundation garment now found only in fetish magazines, and unlike my mom, she always seemed to be wearing a girdle. Bright lipstick, an ash-blonde bouffant, and pointy high heels completed the look.

Roberta liked men and cultivated any brand of male attention, even that of a twelve-year-old. If she caught me lurking around the kitchen, she offered me a cold drink or a snack instead of shooing me out to play with the other kids. Maybe she just felt sorry for me, pitying my shyness. And my fascination with Roberta was only rivaled by my infatuation with her daughter. Debbie Gilchrist was to my eyes perfection, a petite girl with fair skin and long dark hair, full lips, and deep brown eyes under heavy lids that gave her the air of a bored, detached princess.

Certainly Roberta could see that I was thoroughly smitten, and in an uncharacteristic act of generosity had offered to bake a special cake for me on my last birthday. Instead of the usual sugary white slab studded with plastic cowboys and Indians, her creation was something I had never before seen. It was magnificent: three layers of the deepest chocolate bound together with coconut-laced goo. More goo was slathered the top, oozing enticingly over the edges, and as she carried it into the room, her face was lit flatteringly by twelve slim blue candles.

"What kind is it, Mrs. Gilchrist?"I asked, my wide eyes taking in the voluptuous concoction.

"German Chocolate," she said.

I imagined it a rare confection, only available in the pastry shops of Old Europe. It was my first adult cake.

Later that spring, plans got underway for the big event of our church year. The Easter service was to be organized around a cantata and pageant, of which the focal point would be a rustic cross, life-sized, set up in the front of the sanctuary. At the climax of the music, a real crown of thorns was to be hung reverently on the cross, and the congregation would file forward and place flowers at its foot. There was much discussion by the ladies of the pageant committee as to the important role of hanging the crown. It should be a girl, they decided. There was the pretty little Hollingsworth girl but she was a bit young—there was no sense in taking a risk that she might prick herself on the thorns and cry, or heaven forbid, drop the crown. Then there were a couple of other likely girls, both older. But they sang in the choir, and would be needed there. Debbie Gilchrist would be perfect.

The choir rehearsed for weeks, nearly wearing out the director, Miss Kingsbury, and the organist, Carolyn Sue Eubanks. On the Saturday prior, some of the men went into the woods and brought back two straight sweet gum trunks with the bark left on, then hacked out notches like Lincoln Logs and assembled them into the giant cross. By four that afternoon it loomed impressively at the head of the center aisle. I was one of four boy ushers, our job to pass trays of blossoms down each pew, supplying the floral tribute. The ladies of the missionary society had covered cardboard shirt boxes with aluminum foil, and a half-inch of water kept the azalea and bridal wreath crisp and sweet, their odors mingling with the spicy sharpness of the freshly oiled pews and waxed pine floors.

By 10:30 on Easter morning the church was so full that the older boys had to open the side bay and set up folding chairs for the latecomers. Reverend Mims' deep baritone guided the members through the liturgy, booming out the responsive readings and the familiar story of the Passion. The choir sang like overfed angels, the flower trays were passed, hearts and collection plates were filled to the brim.

At the emotional height of the service, Carolyn Sue steered the organ into a bold rendition of "The Old Rugged Cross," and Debbie entered the sanctuary, walking ever so slowly down the aisle, her eyes on the big cross at the front, the crown balanced carefully on the very tips of her delicate outstretched fingers. All eyes in the congregation, the choir, the pulpit, followed her. Her glossy dark hair was board straight and fell below her shoulders, and at the back of her head a thick hank was held in place by a flat bow of wide velvet ribbon, butter yellow like her dress. It was the perfect Easter dress for a young girl from a nice family: just above the knee, an empire waist ringed with embroidered daisies, long voile sleeves ending in three-button cuffs. Her shoes were low pumps with chunky heels that Roberta had specially dyed to match the dress.

Debbie lifted her arms slowly, gracefully, as she neared the cross, her hemline inching just slightly up her thighs. She found the nail in the center and hung the crown without fumbling, then modestly took her seat in the front pew. From my place a few feet away I watched the rest of the congregation step forward, row by row, and place their flowers at the foot of the cross. Many an eye was wet with emotion, lips trembled, but Roberta's face was serene, placid, her pride just barely subdued.

When the service ended, the adults gathered in the fellowship hall for coffee and cookies, the children left to themselves out in the bright April sunshine. Several of us boys always lingered in the sanctuary, helping clean up the discarded programs and crackly cellophane candy wrappers left behind by the worshippers. I stacked the flower trays, still holding their water and a few picked-over flowers, and headed out the back door of the church. Just as I dumped the water into the weeds behind the churchyard fence, I caught a flash of yellow past the corner of the building.

Quietly, I slipped along the wall until I reached the corner and peeked around. In an angle formed by a wing of the church, Debbie stood with her back to me. Her skirt was high enough on one side to show a triangle of white panty, and over her shoulder, red and bloated against her sleek dark hair, was the face of Kurt Melder, the meanest boy in school. A sheen of sweat covered his forehead and his eyes were squeezed shut as if in pain. And below, I could see Debbie's slim, pale wrist working up and down, her hand inside the fly of his dark wool pants.

Before I could clear out, Kurt spotted me.

"Get the hell away from here you little sissy!" he spat.

I had already turned away.

Years later I apologized to my mother for what I'd said in front of the mirror that day. I was surprised to hear that she didn't remember a bit of it, but I still felt the sting of my disloyalty.

I asked her about Roberta Gilchrist. They'd lost touch years before but my mom still saw Debbie occasionally, working at the Walgreens photo counter.

"Roberta was a bitch," Mom said, "but I felt sorry for her. Her husband ran around on her, and she'd had a couple of nervous breakdowns while they were living overseas."

"But what about that cake?" I asked. "The German Chocolate one she made for my twelfth birthday?"

"Oh yeah, that cake," she recalled."It was out of a box."

Bad Impressions

Dan Mancuso

Tact. It is, arguably, one of the more important aspects of a social individual. I say *arguably* because I am the epitome of tactlessness and yet I have gotten along fine, perhaps because I don't realize my faux pas until a week later. For example, I once had a very one-sided conversation about how obnoxious the French are with a French citizen. It wasn't until I walked away that I realized his reason for disagreement. It's unfortunate, but true, to say that that was one of my more politically correct moments.

This, on the other hand, was not. I received an invitation to a friend's house for dinner, to which I responded with much enthusiasm, as any right-minded teenage boy would, seeing as food was involved. We were all sitting around the dinner table, enjoying a nice family meal when the conversation somehow turned to the gay individual who works with one of my friend's parents. This then began a conversation about the surprisingly large number of homosexual people there are. With an attempt at a dumb joke, "Sheesh, everybody's gay these days." I successfully shut everybody up. It took me only a moment to realize why nobody was talking: My friend's sister was gay, and sitting across from me. What's worse was that her "partner" was sitting right next to her, and they were in the act of feeding each other. It only took a moment for my friend to lean over and whisper, "Yeah, their right under your nose!" Fortunately for me it was a cheerful crew, and they decided not to boot me out of the house, at least not yet.

I had lucked out that time, but I am afraid my filterless mouth might have gotten me in trouble. Just before school started I was walking the campus to try and figure out where my classes were, seeing as it was my first year at HVCC and I didn't know where anything was. During my wanderings, one nice lady asked if I was lost. I told her I was simply walking through my schedule, and she responded what a good idea that was. She then introduced herself as the Dean of Liberal Arts and offered to help. I was taken aback because, unless I'm mistaken, being the dean of anything is usually a big deal. Anyways, she asked to see my schedule, so I showed it, pointing out that I'm in the engineering program. So the top three classes, Chemistry, Calculus, and Engineering Tools, were my focus. Below those classes were College Forum, First Aid, and English, which I pointed at and said, "These on the other hand, their just fluff." I now understand that I am going to fail English because I told the Dean of Liberal Arts that it is a "fluff" class.

Perhaps tact is an important part to a well-rounded individual. It is a difficult problem to address though because the person I'm speaking to is always too speechless to retort. So unless a friend is nearby to tell me what I just said, I'll keep going about my day as if I just had a wonderfully pleasant conversation. Or I'll not worry about it and let my mouth keep rampaging until I do get kicked out of somebody's home.

Scene Four: Queen Charlotte's Ball from "A Fool Such as I"

Sarah O'Connor Filippelli

It's late in the evening on an unseasonably warm spring night in 1959. The windows in the apartment are mostly open allowing a breeze to occasionally slip inside teasing those into thinking that for a moment they were comfortable. Cars driving past can be heard like gentle waves rolling onto the shore of a beach, until occasionally a large truck goes by and the entire apartment building tremors under the passing vehicle's weight. A RCA "fliptop" TV hums in the background, its pictures projecting rolling shadows across the living room walls. There are no lights on in the room making it nearly impossible to see. The only source of light is the glow from the black-and-white television that stands in the far corner of the room. During a particularly bright scene playing on the television, the room is momentarily illuminated. We see that there is a couch pressed tightly against the wall across from the TV behind a low table and sandwiching the couch is an armchair and small love seat. Squeezed against one arm of the couch, we notice a small body wrapped in a large white bedsheet leaving only their face and feet visible. The room goes dark as the television's program changes scenes. We hear movement from outside the apartment. Scuffing on the ground and keys jingling simultaneously. The front door to the apartment opens, light from the hallway rushes in. A shadow of a man is visible; it's Robert.

Robert: (*You can tell he is noticeably irritated without seeing his face. He rips the keys from the lock and throws them into the darkness obviously aiming for nothing.*) Dammit Jane.

(*He flicks on the light switch located alongside the front door. The living room lights up.*)

What is this you're watching? More of this Fred Astaire and Ginger Rogers fairytale dream livin'?

(*He walks forcefully toward Jane, inching his way into her view. She blinks twice deliberately as to adjust her eyes to the light. She stares are him glossily and wide-eyed. The sheet is still wrapped tightly over her head, her hands grasping at it from the inside pulling it taught over her knuckles. Its whiteness makes her features even more porcelain and blue eyes more piercing.*)

I come home to you, (*fails his arms*) you wrapped up like some mummy! (*Narrows his eyes at her*) Are you even listening?

(*She nods, loosening her grip on the sheet. It falls around her shoulders like a cape. Her red hair is wild with strands sticking up haphazardly most likely from static.*)

The men I know they come home to dinner. I don't even come home to lights.

(*Jane glances past Robert to the television. As she does this Robert turns his attention to the TV. His tone of voice changes and suddenly appears hurt and confused.*)

What are you watching?

Jane: (*She sits up in the couch and looks at Robert.*) It's just some coverage of a debutant ball.

Robert: (*He looks back at the television then back at her. He starts to walk to Jane but pauses.*) Is that what this is about?

Jane: What's what about?

Robert: (*As though he had expert knowledge*) This whole bit. You know dolly we had that once, real big time just like in those flicks.

(*Jane casts her eyes down at her toes. Robert moves in and kneels to be in her sight.*)

And I'm not sayin' we lost it. You've just been difficult Jane and it's taken a toll on me.

Jane: (*Apologetically*) I wasn't trying to be difficult.

Robert: Most people don't try to be difficult, but as close as I want to be to you there are things a man's got to do for himself. I can't lose this job.

Jane: (*Interjecting*) But you said when you came home…

Robert: (*Strongly*) I said "when I come home" because I didn't know if I was comin' home Jane. I wasn't going to write you some letter about how I figured I would die out there in some jungle and that if I was lucky perhaps maybe my body might make it home. I wrote you letters to keep myself inspired and your letters kept me alive, but do you know how many other men were out there gettin' letters from their woman back at home and died? Do you?

Jane: No.

Robert: Well a lot. Have I ever lied to you?

Jane: No.

Robert: We got married didn't we?

Jane: Yes, but…

Robert: This whole bit about the baby. There's nothing sayin' we won't ever have all them little ones you want. We can try again. (*He looks at Jane sincerely.*) And again. And again. Maybe we can try even if it's just for the hell of it. (*Jane smiles.*) Now that's progress.

(*He touches her chin with his fingers and pulls her in to kiss her softly. Their faces not more than inches apart. He grabs Jane's hands and exuberantly pulls her up. Jane is shocked by this sudden movement but is seemingly excited by his energy. He motions back to the television dramatically with his right hand.*)

Robert: (Acting in character) Now I've been to places very exotic, but I must say your beauty astounds me, Miss…?

Jane: (*With flirtatious hesitation*) Miss Jane Ginger

Robert: (*Interjecting*) Who's Ginger?

Jane: (*Sarcastically*) Ginger Rogers

Robert: (*Laughs*) Well then, Miss Jane Ginger, may I have this dance?

Jane: (*She uses the sheet to curtsy.*) Yes, but to whom do I owe this dance?

Robert: (*Matter-of-factly*) Robert. I mean… (*More in character*) Sgt. Robert Harmen.

(*He takes her hand and begins the waltz in the small living room.*)

Jane: (*She places her head on his shoulder and softly mutters.*) What would you do if I really was a Miss?

Robert: Well than I'd have to go and marry you before some other fellow came stealin' you away. Doesn't matter much anyways, because you're my Mrs. Ain't no Ginger about it.

(*The scene ends.*)

Edge of a Secret

Emily Gandron

I looked down at Will's sleeping body, feet touching the soft rug laid out on the floor. His short, wavy hair was tousled from tossing and turning. Wearing only a pair of old grey boxers, my clothes were strewn along with his on the floor. My mind was full of turmoil, guilt, and shame as realization hurled to the forefront of my thoughts. *What had I done?* I pictured Will's honest, brown eyes when he noticed that I had left. They would search around the room even though he already knew what had happened. A sharp pain stabbed my chest at the thought of being the cause of that hurt. What kind of person could I call myself if I stole away like some thief caught stealing? A coward is what I would be, even though countless times people said I was such a hero, such a great role model. Being the star football player at the high school, it was only natural I assumed that role. But who would want some fag as a role model for their kids? I was disgusting, a freak who deceived himself and abhorred his own damn reflection.

The bed made no noise when I struggled to my feet, head hanging in utter shame. Hardly thinking and in a haze, I collected my clothing from the floor, now freezing without the rug underneath my feet. My eyes averted Will's quietly snoring form, unable to even glance at him one more time. Pulling on my worn jeans, I silently whispered, "I'm so sorry." Over and over. It was meaningless to even do something considered so stupid by a lot of people, but I felt compelled even when he couldn't hear me.

My shoes seemed even more difficult to put on than usual as I silently hopped from one foot to another. A few times I almost fell and would have had I not caught myself on Will's overly populated desk. It held a massive heap of papers and books, many of which were covered in a thick layer of dust. His creative home he called it, the place where he could disappear and gather his thoughts. "No rules or judgmental people" he claimed. "God," I thought to myself, "If such a place existed, I would never be in this fucking mess."

Tugging on a shirt that read some long ago name of a forgotten band, I ran my fingers through my disheveled hair. It felt greasy and in need of a wash. Any other time I might have been bothered even a little, but lately I had been letting myself go.

I needed to get the hell out of there. This was my fault in the first place. If I hadn't taken liquor from my parent's cabinet, I wouldn't have gotten so messed up and come to the party that landed me with the one person I avoided so hard in school. He plagued my thoughts constantly, and nothing could make me stop wanting to see him. Will was from another social group and often the butt of jokes. I never really took part in that stuff, and when I did, it was so I didn't look like I cared. There were so many times I knew he heard my friends. He never said a word back to any of them, but I believed whenever he glanced up that he was silently forgiving me. That's what made the whole thing seem inhuman.

Within an hour I had stolen from Will's house and reached my small truck where it was parked next to the curb. Sliding behind the wheel, my eyes just stared at the keys lying in my hand. They laid heavy in my palm; like me they were cold and lifeless. Nothing could change. All of this, like so many other times, would be erased and never spoken of again. I eventually got myself to start the car. My eyes scanned Will's house one more time, half hoping he'd be awake and come out to stop me.

I gunned the engine and sped off for school. Sam would be there by now, engulfed in her typical routine of swimming laps around the pool. To keep on the swim team, she'd get up early to take a couple laps around the pool three times a week. Fat, that's what she always said about herself. It seemed just about every other week she was on some new diet. I tried to picture her flame-colored hair, drenched from the pool. How it clung a little down her slender shoulders and dripped water which pooled around her feet. Her cornflower blue eyes would be bright from the exertion used to get through the exercise. They'd shine, vigilant of their surroundings.

Nothing came to me as I envisioned Sam in my thoughts, trying desperately to unearth something. I was considered the luckiest guy in our school for being able to nail the hottest chick. But I didn't consider myself anything but unlucky. Every part was played to perfection in our school. As the star football player, I naturally was dating one of the greatest looking girls there. However, that's not what I ached for. It appeared everything was planned for me. My father expected me to go to college and become a lawyer—some family tradition he couldn't live down. Mother wanted me to eventually settle down with a girl and give her grandkids.

I looked up at myself through the rearview mirror and could see the tears pricked at the corner of my eyes. Did I regret lying to myself every day? No, not if it kept my family together and allowed things to stay the same. Will would never wait for me. What right would I have to ask him? But would this charade which dances on my strings turn into my own downfall?

Worth the Sandwich?

Rebecca Vitarelle

We've all heard it before: "Honey, could you make me a sandwich?" Make a sandwich, fetch a beer, whatever it may be, and every time we women roll our eyes, sigh, and think about what it would be like to be single. Or maybe you are a single lady longing to hear that question, though I'd doubt it. Regardless, maybe it's time we take a really big step back and think, "Is he really worth making the sandwich?"

Single women are as free as migratory geese; they can fly in whatever gaggle they wish and squawk at whichever and however many males they please. It's an empowering sensation women feel that is often admired and envied by others. Not being "tied down" to any one particular person allows the single woman to do whatever she pleases with her spare time, be it hanging out with friends, shopping, being bored, or even hunting down a significant other. However, spending time with friends and doing other activities can also mean spending copious amounts of money. When being single, it's not frequent that women get a reprieve from paying for all of their activities, and pay for themselves. Occasionally, there may be a date or a courteous friend who puts forth some cash for her pleasure, but this is infrequent. Single women, while lacking money, may also be lacking in the cuteness we crave as women. Friends are not cute; we love them, but they do not fill our cute quota. Family is not cute either; actually, more frequently than not, family is annoying. To get the cuteness fill, single women search out chick flicks, puppies, or babies to fill their gap. This can be a good thing though, as this allows women to have full control over their cuteness intake so as not to make themselves sick with or annoyed by adorability.

After a case like that, most women would start to pack up the bread and boot the boy, but I wouldn't suggest it quite yet. Women with a male significant other, those who are "taken," are not quite as free as single women. They do have their partner to think about when making decisions, especially when it comes to flirting or hanging out with male friends, and some relationships are a bit more constricting than others. This restriction may further irritate the taken woman. However, this is to be expected; we sometimes forget that if we switched we would not be pleased with our men ogling other women. In reality, it's a protective measure for the good of the relationship. But why? Unlike single women, the taken woman frequently has a way to spend her free time: with the beau. A lot of time is spent with him so she never has to be bored or lonely, unless she feels like she needs time away to be alone or with the girls. In this sense there is always a loyal companion to spend time with. Another one of the most wonderful traits that come with having a male significant other is the sudden fattening of the wallet. Most, if not all, of the activities together will be paid for by him. Even if the female is stubborn and intent on paying, the male is usually more stubborn and will win the battle. Women just have to remember, of all the battles to lose, that's the best one. Women should also remember this is a gesture made from chivalry and sweetness. When boy pays for shared activities, it does not mean he thinks the girl is incapable of doing so, he's just trying to be sweet. The sweet or silly acts that boyfriend or hubby sporadically commit for her are the same acts she fawned over in books or on the silver screen as a single lady. Part of the role of beau is to be cute, be it through surprises or sayings, and we women love it, because it allows us to feel loved.

So, unpack the lunch meat taken ladies, because you know deep down inside of yourself that making him a sandwich is a gesture of your love and appreciation for him. There are times he drives you crazy, but he does a lot for you, and he means well. For all the single ladies out there, go squawk at a few more guys before you migrate to "taken-land." A few loaves of bread may go stale before you find that special guy, but when you do, it'll be worth it.

Society Is a Casket

Kaitlyn Tate

I am the pastry of the supermarket.
From behind the casket of glass
I see the fresh fruits, brilliantly organic.
They don't see that I am trapped here;
my captivity is transparent.
They willingly grew themselves
and I had no say in what I became.
They sit freely bare in their open cartons;
my original color had been stripped away.
I was not appealing in my old skin,
so they brushed over me red, tan, and brown.
It is important that I appeal to others;
that is how a pastry is chosen.
I did not ask for this upon myself
though no one would be able to hear me
from behind my closed casket of glass.

The World through a Window

Paige Farrara

The sound of a gavel slamming on hardwood. This and the accompanying visual are what most of us think of when we think of court. My experiences with it have been a little different than that. More along the lines of hushed voices, rustling papers, and family melodramas unfolding in fluorescently lit courtrooms that look nothing like they do on television. My own personal drama began on a hot summer day in the beginning of August with a phone call from my mother. It was a kind of sticky hot that always makes me feel unclean, no matter how many cold showers I take or how many times I go swimming. It has always seemed amazing to me how much one phone call can change the course of your entire life. How many countless families have answered their phones to be devastated by the news that there's been an accident, or a family member has been hurt in the line of duty, etc.? My news was not nearly as serious, but it was nonetheless devastating and hit like a right hook straight to my gut.

It was two days after my eighteenth birthday and I could hardly believe the words that my mom was saying. "I got a letter from family court; your father is petitioning to stop child support payments and to remove you from his health insurance..." The words rang hollow and buzzed through my head, making me dizzy. I sat down on the cracked, crumbling concrete front steps and hung onto the railing as if it might support me, as if it might stop the tears from coming. My father, whose pittance of a weekly check and health insurance were the closest thing to love I'd received from him in eighteen years on this planet, was filing to stop those. The worst part, to me at least, was how absolutely unfair it seemed. I was living in the basement of my ex-stepfather's house, working part-time at Price Chopper and earning barely enough to put gas in my car. Beyond that, I had pre-existing mental health conditions that would make obtaining coverage nearly impossible. But that was my father.

In eighteen years on this planet, I could remember only one time when my father told me that he loved me. I was eight years old, lying in a hospital bed before I went into surgery. That horrible, sterile hospital smell clung to everything and the phone call was short. "I love you, Bud." And then the anesthesiologist asked me to count backward from ten. "Ten, nine, eight…" I don't think I got any further than that before the silver operating room began to spin and the world went dark. Eighteen years and I could remember each time he had embraced me as a child, because the occurrences were so few and far between. It was easier still to remember the harshness of his actions. The sting of a hand to my cheek after I dared to refer to my stepfather as "Dad." The sting of his harsh words as I made yet another childish mistake. At this point, it had been nearly two years since I'd given up on my father, two years since we'd last spoken, and yet despite this time passed, the sting of this new brand of rejection felt just as strong as ever.

The next two months passed by in a haze of drug-induced numbness. Each summer day and night blended into the next as I searched for everything, anything to dull the pain. Memories of a cornfield and fireworks at midnight blend into clutching the ugly brown fibers of a seventies-style shag carpet as the room spun hopelessly before me. Then, suddenly, it was October and unseasonably warm, and the date of the family court appearance had arrived. Although I wanted to be present for the court session, I was banished to the waiting room for what seemed like an eternity. The wooden benches in the waiting room were dark wood, polished to perfection, and cold as ice. My mother emerged from the courtroom first, a victorious smile on her face that clearly conveyed that we had "won." My father exited next, looking chunky in his maroon polo shirt and Wranglers blue jeans. For a second, I almost recognized his blonde hair and blue eyes as my own flesh and blood. I shouted across the court waiting room to him, eighteen years of pent up emotions welling up in me. "I hope you know that this is all your fault. Everything that has ever happened to me has been because of you!" I will never forget the smirk that crossed his face, starting in one corner of his ugly mouth and traveling to the other. His stupid, short-sleeve polo-clad arm bent as he elbowed his lawyer, laughed, and muttered something unintelligible to me. That was it. Eighteen years of pain and anguish and hospital stays, of stitches, of blood, of tears, of pills and razor blades and hunger, and he laughed like it was a private joke.

My stomach dropped a dozen stories on an elevator from hell, and I wanted to fall to the ground. My mother, however, gripped my arm and led me out of the courtroom. Her high heels clicked together across the cold tile floors, sounding much more confident than I felt. We exited the building back into the warmth of that October day, the sky blue and the street lined in vibrant green trees. As I sunk into the dark leather of the passenger seat of my mom's car. I knew it was over. This private hell that he had been cultivating for my entire life was over. We had won. I turned my head and did not look back, and I haven't looked back since.

The Sun Slowly Rises over a Conscript

E. J. McCormick

The fields to my front taunt me. They remind me how far I am from home. They look so surreal and haunting. I want nothing more than the November sun.

The grapevines rest, leaning on berms maniacs have tilled through the land. The rows run every direction. A patchwork of earth, the dirt piled twice a man's height is a maze that farmers constructed. I sit and I stare to the distance, while the breeze chills and blows through the trees. The vines wave stick fingers toward me, leafless now that November has come.

I crouch staring at this world before me… painted in khaki, tan, and brown. If not for the blue of the cold sky, I would not believe colors existed here at all. The autumn has robbed the last grapevines of green. Only stringy brown tendrils remain. Branches crest mound after mound, casting shadows on the embankments and mimic the matted locks of the insane. The breeze comes again and bites at my skin; the dead vines wave, and invite me to join them. Vines so lifeless but warmed in the sun.

I cover myself in a blanket, a gray of January skies filled with driving ice, snow, and frost. Here there is only the latter, in late November, and miles from home. On the trench works that face me, built by farmers, the grapes long plucked from the vines, the sun dances on berms and weaves through the rows, but on me, shadows only will come.

In the field, a grape house sits lonely, like a brick fallen from some giant's hand. Vertical slits cut through its walls, like a hundred of the blackest eyes. I wish I could see what was behind it, wish I knew what lay inside. At harvest, the grapes are gathered, when the hottest orb burns bright in the sky. Here they don't know of Grappa or Riesling, but only the wrath of the sun. Millions of grapes change to raisins when brought to the grape huts and hung.

It's November, and the harvest long over. Every last raisin had its time in the sun. The grape huts constructed from man's sweat, straw, and clay become giant blocks of Panjwai adobe. Between harvests, the huts are never lonely. There is always work to be done. The slits that stare at me, an army of vacant dark voids, are just the right size for a gun.

In my blanket of gray I am crouching, propping myself and machine gun on a mud wall. I sit silent and stare at the trench works. I try to peer through the grape hut's dark soul. But it is really the sun, the warm sun, I am watching. It moves closer still, but remains just out of reach, because another grape hut's shadow pours over me. The sun and its warmth become just a tease. November's chill air gnaws my fingers, while the sour dust chokes at my nose. This strange land is so foreboding, but the autumn sun reminds me of home.

So the fields to my front only taunt me. They remind me how far I am from home. They are hostile as fangs on a viper. I want nothing more, than the November sun.

Panjwai, you'll never take me… no matter how strongly you call. You can wave your dead branches in welcome. Your grape huts can wink their black eyes. Panjwai, you know I'll leave you. To every foreigner you've always said your goodbyes, whether they were carried off your grape-mounds by comrades or walked from your fields on their own.

Camping

Chad Coumbes

Camping. Every American dreams of spending restless, wakeful nights in the open outdoors, combating wildlife and fending off starvation. I too have endured hardships, but none can truly be compared to the awfulness of the outdoors! Do not misconstrue my words. I have great admiration toward those who make the otherwise passé experience that is camping seem effortless and fun. I am a man of technology. I am a man who would rather observe the stars in an undisturbed, *safe* location; a location far removed from the bewilderment that nature may present. Do not misconstrue my words, though. I have the deepest respect for the great outdoors! If nature had intended us to continue down the path of uncivil, primal life, we would not be having this discussion.

We all enjoy the comforts in modern day society all too well. Why struggle to boil water in order to purge it of contaminants when you could turn but one knob and enjoy crisp, clean water in a matter of seconds? Is it a thing of curiosity to prove to ourselves that we're capable of withstanding the wrath of Gaea herself?

Again, do not misconstrue my words. I do enjoy the simple things in life, after all. I just prefer to not face the agony that is camping outdoors. Why ruin a perfectly comfortable bed; ruin an easily obtainable source of food in the refrigerator; ruin the time with the toilet that is eager to service? Why take for granted these otherwise overlooked luxuries? I say the idea of camping is open for interpretation, subjective if you will. The next time you feel the urge to camp, instead, consider your home a camp and eagerly await the forgone atrocities in comfort.

Getting to Where I'm Going

Lana Medina

August 2001—the world was a place of relative security, at least in the minds of many Americans. One could travel through airport security with a small pocket knife, with liquids greater than three ounces, and with one's shoes and dignity on. When my family embarked on our trip to Italy, we had no worries except what city to explore first. Although we would be spending our vacation in Italy, my family decided to land in Brussels, Belgium, and drive via Germany, Austria, and Switzerland to reach Italy. The culture of Europe was about to explode on my mind and I was eager to soak up as much of it as possible.

In Germany, the first city we visited was Trier. This city, at one time, was occupied by the Romans, and ruins from their empire can still be visited today. From our home-like bed and breakfast, we walked to visit a nearby Roman amphitheater. My brother and I conducted an experiment to understand the powers of this structure. We went to opposite sides of the arena and began whispering to each other. The conversation was not only crystal clear, but audible to a person standing anywhere in the amphitheater. It was as if we were right next to each other. Standing in the midst of this massive architectural marvel, it was not hard for the mind's eye to imagine what events occurred when under Roman control. Towering rows of stone seats surround you; lions pace anxiously in dark, damp underground chambers; adrenaline pulsates through the veins of spectators; and, as if by supernatural powers, your voice thunders over the noisy, rowdy crowd as you announce the start of the exhibition. It was hard to believe that this amphitheater was built by hand.

After this interesting detour, we arrived at the city of Lindau after midnight. This beautiful island city is located on Lake Constance. A lighthouse and statue of a lion rests lightly off shore and create a beautiful picturesque scene. The next day we strolled through the town and admired its quiet beauty. We then departed Lindau and traveled through a long tunnel to Austria. As soon as we exited the tunnel, our car broke down, and we had to get out and push it to the side of the road. Unfortunately, this particular town was having a festival that day, and many of the businesses were closed. However, DAK, the German version of AAA, was able to tow us to their mechanic shop. They discovered that we had not run out of gasoline, but rather had too much of it! My father had mistakenly put gasoline in our vehicle, not observing that it ran on diesel. Thankfully, the mechanic was able to fix the problem in a few hours; in the meantime I had managed to lock myself in the bathroom. Just a few turns of a screwdriver fixed that problem, and we were off once more.

That evening we arrived in Switzerland and stayed in the town of Bellinzona, near the border of Italy. Although we had planned on arriving in Italy that night, the car trouble forced us to make this detour. This change in plans afforded us the opportunity to enjoy a nice dinner. All was going well at this impromptu feast until my brother cut his hand when he crushed a wine glass. The next morning we decided to explore the city. Bellinzona has an extensive city wall and castle known as the Castelgrande. The stone castle wall was wide and had crucifix shaped openings, where archers could attack the enemy but still be protected. There was a theater production that day inside the castle. I was too shy to ask for a picture with the cast, so my father requested it on my behalf. I am still curious why they were dressed in Egyptian garb!

The next day we arrived in Italy, and it was hot! Mount Etna was active, and most days it reached 100 degrees Fahrenheit. Before we could enjoy the beautiful mountains and endless sunflower fields, we had to make one stop. My grandmother was in dire need of a rest room, so we left the expressway and drove to the closest town. Little did we know that we would drive in to what could be the Italian equivalent of an American ghost town. That is to say, the town was dead. After a few eerie moments, we located a public bathroom. Shortly after my grandmother walked in, she came tumbling back out doubled over in riotous laughter. It took her fifteen minutes to calm down enough to tell us what had happened. She proceeded to tell us that what one person calls a toilet, another calls a hole in the ground. Literally, it was a hole in the floor with two impressions on either side of the hole to indicate where one's feet should go. After this humorous (and disturbing) event, we arrived at Dracula's castle, or, as it is commonly known, the landlady's villa. The landlady led us to a beautiful, rustic farmhouse in the countryside of San Andrea di Sorbello in Niccone Valley. Down the dirt road from our farmhouse, a woman was giving horseback riding lessons. The caramel-colored horse I rode was named Felix. I learned tricks such as standing on the horse, riding backward on the horse, lying down on the horse, performing a trick nicknamed the "superman" on the horse, and riding bareback on the horse. Those lessons inspired my passion for all things equestrian.

Every day we traveled to different cities. Assisi, Gubbio, Spoleto, Deruta, Citta di Castello, Pisa, Catiglione del Lago, Rome, Preggio, Perugia, and Florence all bear our footprints. Each city holds many memories. I leave with this thought: Experience something amazing and memorable with people you love. I had that experience, and I hope I always have as much fun in life as when I was "getting to where I was going."

Circumventing Circumlocution

Paul Hunter

Words are sought
to block
feelings that are revealing.
They become an obstruction to substance,
an obstacle to meaning,
and with each repeated guess
they can mean more, or skew toward meaning-less;
there is added stress with each attempt to question
and compare the symmetry with previous suggestions
various veils of suspension,
cognitive dissension,
a possible deception...
Are you getting closer to the truth with each thing mentioned
or is it lies you're becoming more entrenched in?
Sometimes it's hard to decide each mind's intention;
you think you're getting closer to the right view,
then something comes and takes it out from under you.
They could be saying it, just to trouble you,
or maybe even discover you,
but how would you know
if you're not accustomed to
this something new,
and you're left thinking
are they saying something or
doing nothing but befuddling you?
With just words it always ends up open to review,
which is why an ounce of action is worth a ton of truth.

Childhood Terrors

Romey Romano

We all have them, childhood memories that borderline on terrors. They are terrifying at the time and turn out to be funny years later. Here are just two of the many stories from my childhood. Both vignettes took place before my seventh birthday.

Boat Ride

Every August the St. Joseph's Catholic Church in Chester, Vermont, had a fair to raise money for the parish. The one-acre field behind the church was divided in half. On the left side St. Joseph's Church had booths with homemade foods, and games of chance like ring toss and spinning wheels. They also had a huge, for a seven-year-old, musty tent that they used as a bingo hall.

The other half of the field was rented to a traveling show that had small kiddie amusement park rides and trailers that sold fried dough, cotton candy, and other delicacies. One of the rides is a bit hard to explain. It featured boats that were painted blue or red. Each boat had two rows of seats holding two children each. At each seat there was a cast metal wheel that resembled a boats helm and a pair of light chains that acted as rudimentary seat belts. Each boat rode on two wheels that were in line with the keel that were guided by a *U*-shaped channel of steel. This channel formed a circle around the center pole and had a series of hills and valleys that mimicked the waves of the sea.

My father seated me and my sister in our blue boat. There was a little bell at the bow with a pull string. My sister held the string and while we both had wheels, I was the skipper. The boy in the next boat was wiggling around in his seat, obviously overdosing on cotton candy and other treats. Before my father left us to our voyage he glanced at the kid in the boat ahead and said to us, “Have fun but don’t horse around.”

So the ride starts. I’m steering, my sister’s ringing the little bell, and we’re waving to our folks each time we pass by. The second or third time around I felt a bump-bump and then there was screaming. I don’t remember if there was a second set of bumps. I do remember the ride stopping and my father undoing our chain seatbelts.

The boy that had been riding in the boat in front of us was with his parents. He was crying and had two vertical red lines across his forehead and left cheek from the wheel channel. My father said, “See what happens when you horse around.”

The kid’s parents were leading him away, and just like the Bugs Bunny show, there was a black tire track running down his back.

Fishing

Growing up Catholic I was taught that all snakes were evil, and thus I equated them with anything that wriggled on the ground, this including worms and caterpillars.

My family had traveled from southeastern Vermont to eastern Connecticut to visit my mom’s side of the family. While there, as an extended family group, we went to some sort of campground that was either owned by a relative or was used for the day. The pond’s water was root beer colored, probably had a high rust content, and would turn your legs brown if you stayed in the water too long. There were tons of cattails and a sandy beach with a weather beaten boathouse and dock. There was also a grassy beach where our collective parents set up all us kids with fishing rods.

Not wanting to touch the evil snakelike worm, my father baited my hook. God knows what we would have caught in that pond besides leaches, ringworm, or a case of diarrhea. I plunked my worm in the water and waited for a strike.

My father then baited my younger sister Nicole's hook. She is almost three years younger than me, making her about four at the time. My father told her to put the line in the water. She must have watched too many fishing shows with my Grandpa Brodeur, 'cause she whipped the fishing pole back and then forward to launch her worm into the pond.

The worm didn't go to the deep six, instead the line had wrapped around my right calf. I looked down and saw the fishing line, hook, and gooey bleeding worm wrapped tightly around my calf and let out a scream. Not just a scream, but a little boy whose voice hasn't changed yet scream.

At first my father thought I was bleeding from the hook, but luckily for him, it was worm blood.

And now, years later, and over a half a dozen shrinks later, on the bright side, I can rescue worms if I steel myself for the touch of their clammy little bodies. However, I still cannot bait a hook or go on rides that go in a circle, unless it is a Ferris wheel.

A Moment That Felt Like Eternity

Kylie Maunu

Thirty seconds on a cold, snowy night in January changed the way I felt about the way my generation parties. With adolescence comes a false sense of invincibility. When you hear about overdoses and alcohol poisonings or other out-of-hand situations, it's usually because you're watching it on the news, reading about it in a magazine, or being forced to watch some low-budget, outrageous health video that nobody seems to take serious enough. The only thing that will provide enough shock-value to really shake a person up is experience.

It was the weekend and it was time to party; fortunately for me, although I didn't know it was a good thing at the time, it was my turn to be the designated driver for the night. Considering I was the only one who experienced it completely sober, my memory of it is the clearest. A group of my friends and I headed toward the boondocks to satisfy our craving for "fun." We were, at very least, fifteen minutes away from any sort of civilization and that includes hospitals. I was sitting at a round, wooden table in a cigarette-smoke–filled screen room that was uncomfortably packed with people just like the ashtray was uncomfortably packed with cigarette butts. Everyone was wearing winter coats, scarves and hats of the sort, trying desperately to stay warm, even though you could see your breath every time you exhaled. As I looked around, I noticed the rosy-pink color of all my friends' noses and cheeks and amongst all the chatter I could hear an occasional sniffle or two as well as the clanking of beer bottles. My friend's gray and rather large dog was running around sniffing everybody, excited and worked up from all the commotion.

Across from me stood my friend, who was extremely inebriated to say the very least. His system was loaded with hallucinogenic magic mushrooms, Coors Light, and "the dankest bud around." He took one last drag of his Marlboro Red, and immediately after he set it down in the ashtray, his eyes rolled into the back of his head. As he collapsed to the ground, a loud snap echoed in the room causing everyone to become silent and utterly confused. I soon realized that his head had caused the loud snap I heard, cracking a broom in half as he went down. He started convulsing on the ground initially, but then he gradually stopped moving. His face was the color of pale pea soup, and he had a terrifyingly lifeless look in his eyes—the kind of look that gets burned into your retinas, one you can never forget. At first I, and everyone else, thought he was dead and this wasn't a movie like we were used to; this was real life.

A few of my friends, including my boyfriend, immediately rushed to his aid and helped him up as he slowly regained semiconsciousness. His face was still a pale green and he ended up losing bladder control, so there was a wet spot in his jeans. It was so hard to look at him without feeling flooding emotions of panic, shock, and heartache. My boyfriend and another one of our close friends helped him outside so that he could get away from the cigarette smoke and get a breath of fresh air. There was no way he could walk on his own for he was blind and mumbling all kinds of nonsense, and trying to lead him was like trying to move dead weight. We threatened our friend that if he didn't get any better in the immediate time following, that we had no choice but to call an ambulance, which we were all terrified of. In the next few minutes, our friend was back to himself again, amazingly and gratefully. After that point, I had locked myself in the bathroom to take it all in and I let myself become engulfed in the true emotions that I couldn't show at first. He ended up being fine—thank God—but it was still life changing.

It was a terrifyingly real night in my memory that I will never, ever, be able to forget; for the image of it is still so vivid. I was so scared for my friend that I vowed, from that day forward, to never put any chemicals in my body the way he did. The consequences could have been way more severe than just a reality check and for that I am forever grateful. I think I speak for everyone who was there that night when I say life is way too precious to be wasted on a preconceived "good time" that could potentially turn out deadly, and you shouldn't have to see it to believe it could happen.

Jason

Candace Knibbs

"Grandpa, look at all the stars!"

"Yes I know. The damn city lights eclipse them. But out here, where the darkness hangs freely you can see them all."

The first time that I went camping with my grandfather was when I was seven. In the beginning of our excursion I thought that I would hate it, so I pouted for the whole day. But when my young eyes saw those stars clearly for the first time I fell in love with the wilderness. Every chance that came to go with him, I eagerly took. I even blew off my friends just to spend a night or two in those dark woods. However, that love dwindled to nothing, like the embers of a fire. As I grew, I made other friends. Friends that enjoyed the convenience and entertainment of technology above all else. As I slowly became them, I began to leave my grandfather and his forest behind. When I reached my late teens I had stopped going camping with him completely.

During my third year in college my grandfather finally convinced me to go camping with him again. While we were there I hardly did anything of use, I mostly complained about not having cell service. Sure, I set up the tent, but Grandpa was the one who gathered the wood for the fire, and lost one of his gloves in the process. It was him who lit the fire and fixed dinner. It was him who kindled the conversations we held those days and nights. In all truth my memory of those three days seem more like a hazy dream then any kind of remembrance.

When I returned to my normal life, it was with full force. Once again leaving my grandfather and his beloved wilderness out of my mind, out of my life. Children never mean to forget about their parents or their grandparents, in fact we don't. We just go on with our lives, believing with all of our heart that they will always be there, for us to go back to. Isn't that true freedom? Elders are always complaining that we think we are immortal; but the truth is we believe so strongly in their immortality that we believe that they hold the power to keep us safe, no matter the circumstance. Though learning otherwise is hard and devastating. A year after our last camping trip, he died.

So there I went, to the woods my grandfather so loved, with his ashes. It was written in his will that he would be cremated and that I would have the duty of scattering some of his ashes about his woods. I did as his written words asked and threw him to the wind. Despite the pain that it brought me to be there, in that shadowed place that gave my grandfather such joy, I decided to stay a few days, for his sake.

I wasn't there more than a few hours when, through the bushes a mouse scurried into my camp site and soon after a red fox came crashing in after it. The mouse had disappeared before the fox could nab it. The fox looked about for a bit, jerking her head back and forth. Though when the fox, who I assumed to be female, saw me she barked and stomped at me. When she was satisfied she ran back to the shadows of the woods.

The next day as I was taking a walk, I kept seeing that fox. She ducked behind the trees and bushes on the path ahead of me. Occasionally she'd look back at me with this playful look in her eyes that bade me to follow her, so I did. She took me deep into the forest and off the human trail to one of her design. At one point I did lose sight of her for a time and was left to my own devices.

As the light began to fade she once again appeared ahead of me and dove into a thicket. I followed her. Beyond the thicket I found a ledge, and below was the she-fox and two kits. The two pups were tumbling about, fighting over a leather glove. Their mother sat with a kind of nobility that is usually only seen in wolves, watching them with serenity. The glove the pups so lovingly played with was the one my grandfather lost more than a year ago.

Mother Nature's Fury

Cayleigh Guild

The sky is a beautiful color of blue,
A cloud free sky.
You never know Mother Nature's next move.

One moment Mother Nature can be calm
And the next moment
She can unleash her fury.
Green becomes the color of the sky.

Big puffy clouds engulf the sky.
Twisting and turning the clouds go:
With a blink of an eye,
The cloud touches the ground.

Rain

Kristin Diodonet

At an apartment complex in the suburbs of Eastern falls, the tenant children huddle under a small brush of trees at the edge of the property. They laze about the ground resembling lizards, basking in the sun, with sun burn on their scorched faces. They are a group of five children total—two boys and three girls. They study the people in the complex, their energy wasted on the sun's rays.

The doorways to the tenant homes are all open saving but the screen doors. The adults lie close to the doors or sit on patio furnishings, sipping their icy sodas. The apartments themselves are small renovated motel buildings with ancient air conditioners and few windows. The air conditioners do very little to help the heat and the air is stifling inside. On the inside of one house, a TV is propped close to the front door. The small man on the screen speaks to those passing by, his voice blaring on through the speakers:

> "It's another hot day here in the Hudson Valley, with temperatures near record highs of 103 degrees. There is an advisory going into effect for our area this afternoon due to the heat wave, so right now we advise all of you to stay inside, drink plenty of water, and if you are heading out, wear an SPF of seventy or more...."

As in defiance, one of the children, Ammar, gets up and walks about. The others scramble up as well, following suit. "Itsssss so hot!" he says. His skin has gone from light almond to milk chocolate tan. The children roam the shade under the roof, taking care not to stand too long in the sun. Ammar's sister Hira plucks idly at a dandelion in her hand. "I wish the ice cream man would come," she says irritably. "He goes to Mountain View and we're only down the street." Kristin, the other girl stops walking. There is a cool trickle down her arm for a moment, cooler than the beads of sweat that fall from her face. She says nothing until another drop hits her again, the clouds overhead casting their dark shadows upon the earth. "It's raining," she says softly, as if considering the thought. The other children stop in a tranquil silence.

Rain pelts the earth in rapid speed. "It's raining, it's raining!" says Alicia, Kristin's younger sister. Whooping and hollering in delight, the children run as fast as they can, allowing the cold drops to pierce their skin. The children open their mouths to sing the rain song. Gurgles of words like "gumdrops," and "raindrops," come haltingly as they soak up the cool water in their dry mouths, as delicious as soda pop and lemonade. The force of the rain causes the gutters of the complex overflow with the force of miniature waterfalls. Excitedly the children name them, feeling much like explorers in a transformed new world. They name waterfalls—famous names like Victoria, Niagara, and Angel Falls. Mohammed, the eldest in the group, looks long at one before naming one Begamganj, after his hometown in Bangladesh.

As they turn the corner, they are met with beams of water. Their fathers have come out with water guns and buckets, teasing the children with youthful twinkles in their eyes. Hira ducks and pulls Kristin into her house, where they grab cups to fill with water. Hira's mother's eyebrows rise at them and the muddy tracks on the floor. The two girls pause for a moment waiting, but she merely erupts into laughter and tells them that she will place buckets of water near the door. The neighbors betray their fathers when they get out, pointing in the direction or their hiding places.

Walking outside, the husband of the young couple across from Kristin's apartment comes out carrying a bottle of shampoo and soap. He stands under one of the waterfalls with his swimming trunks and states he is taking a shower. His skin prickles with goose bumps and he gives a few shouts before immersing himself in it fully. The kids laugh to watch him lather his hair under the gutter, comically indifferent to the rain. Sheila, his wife, comes out to laugh at her husband too, their three-month-old daughter in her arms. The baby giggles at her father's faces with dim blue sky lit eyes. She tries to grab the beads of rain in her chubby fingers, jerking her hand back in surprise.

After clouds break, the world is transformed into a steamy muddled mess. The sky looks as if someone has knocked over a paint kit, but only the bright colors have escaped onto the page. Shades of reds, pinks, oranges, and yellows fill the horizon as the tenants watch the sky. The mothers stand in the doorways calling. "Dinnertime!" And the children wander back toward smells of garlic spaghetti, curried chicken, and hamburgers. They dry off in the doorways of their homes, shouting their goodnights on their way in. Their fathers, surrounded by wisps of smoke, share one last cigarette before heading in.

The Virtue of Growing Younger

Fatima Hussain

I was coming home from school one day when it happened. One moment I was looking out the car window, weary-eyed and bored, and the next moment my eyes lit up and I was excitedly jumping up and down in my seat. I turned to my mother and begged her to tell the driver to stop the car. The tires screeched; the car came to a crashing halt. Upon seeing what it was that had suddenly captured my attention, my mother sighed and said, "Fatima, *when* are you finally going to grow up? You're too old to act like this." The object of my mother's seventeen-year-old daughter's interest was a roadside balloon vendor.

Many people will agree with my mother's words. They will say that all of us must grow out of our youthful habits and interests to become responsible adults who "act their age." That way of thinking is, quite frankly, ludicrous. Growing older and wiser and remaining young and playful at heart are not mutually exclusive concepts. People can become more responsible and sensible about their actions as they age, while still retaining their youthful silliness, sense of humor, joy in life, and ability to appreciate the simpler pleasures of the world—like balloons. People take life too seriously for their own good. They forget to laugh at themselves and at life, and say "it's not that big of a deal." We all need to learn how to grow younger instead of always growing older.

The most funny and interesting people are the ones who somehow manage to integrate their maturity with their "immaturity." An example is a friend of my father's, Uncle S. He is a very reputable doctor, is married, and has five grown children. The first time I met Uncle S, many years ago, I was not sure what to make of him. After a very warm "Hello!" to my family, he ushered us into his living room. Then he settled on the couch, turned on the television, kicked up his feet onto the coffee table, and began to watch cartoons. He truly sat there for an hour watching Looney Tunes. A physician in his late forties, nearly bald, with spectacles so thick that they looked bullet-proof, was chortling while watching Wile E. Coyote chase the Road Runner. My siblings still mock him for his eccentricity, but I admire it. Who cares how childish or frivolous people think his behavior is? He's a good, happy, and successful person.

In my mind, this also conjures up images of people like P. G. Wodehouse and Tim Burton. The former was the writer of a plethora of absolutely hilarious works of literature and the latter is the director of a myriad of films with imaginative and funny plots and settings. Both of them are, in my opinion and many others', brilliant artists and complete geniuses. Humor, imagination, silly antics—these things might define a child in the minds of *some* people, but in reality they define a person with the right balance of wisdom and youth.

Another supposedly childish quality is not taking life seriously. Surprisingly, laughing or joking in even semi-serious situations is frowned upon, even though laughter can be very therapeutic. It truly is the best medicine and a very powerful and healthy psychological coping mechanism. A lot of people fail to realize that you can't always control what life throws at you; after a certain point, it's best to just laugh it off. When there is nothing else that can be done, making fun of your situation is not puerile; it is natural and very consoling.

In tenth grade, I had a history midterm that my best friend and I had put our hearts and souls into preparing for. But the day of the exam, an hour before it started, neither she nor I could remember even the most basic things. We could have panicked, but we didn't. Perhaps we went insane for a few minutes, but suddenly we were laughing uncontrollably. We were looking at each other and pointing at our textbooks through tears of laughter, guffawing at the top of our lungs. Everyone was staring at us with scandalized expressions as we clutched our sides and doubled over from the pain of laughing too hard, but we didn't care. We just giggled as if there were no tomorrow. By the time the exam actually started, we felt relaxed and had laughed the worry out of our systems. We both aced that exam, too. This was the first time that I began to realize that life doesn't always have to be a melodramatic war movie. Sometimes the most infantile instinct is the most effective.

Most of us are programmed, almost from the very moment we are born, to take life very seriously. Everything that we do must have a purpose, a meaning; otherwise, it is useless and we are frittering our lives away. Every victory is a step closer to a "goal," and every defeat is a gallop in the direction of failure. It is no wonder that life today is more stressful than ever before in history. It is high time that we borrowed from the younger perception we used to have. What is there to lose by accepting a little bit of reasonless joy in life? Whether you believe that we were created as a lark by a bored deity, or that we are the waste from an eon old explosion, when you put it like I just did, life is still too random and too short to be so solemn and old about.

So take my advice: Slow down and grow younger. Stop to smell a rose or buy a balloon. Don't have hysterics every time you get a C on a test or don't get that promotion you wanted. Sit down and enjoy a nice meal. Smile at a stranger; buy a kid a lollipop. Laugh and be joyous, because splits in your side are better than creases in your forehead.

Inside a Chat Room with Jonathan Edwards, Benjamin Franklin, and Thomas Paine

Rochel Rubin

BF: Hello. Jonathan. Are you there?

JE: Yes, I am. All logged on and ready to burn.

BF: Did you make it, Thomas?

TP: I am all logged in under my own name and ready to give my own spin. Say, have you two been able to observe that last class at Hudson Valley English class in room ADMN 107? I believe the students were asked to do a project on us. Can you believe that? First we get the luxury to be able to observe the class from cyberspace, and now we get the honor of being a part of their lives two hundred years later.

JE: Yeah, WTF [i]

BF: What do the two of you think will happen in an essay?

JE:[1] I think the students will write about how impacted they were by the fact that they will burn in hell if they do not receive the ultimate in personal gratification by knowing the Lord and that they will write something from my speech like, "They deserve to be cast into hell; so that divine justice never stands in the way, it makes no objection against god's using his power at any moment to destroy them" (426).

BF:[1] Hey, why do you think that religion is the only way they will think? This is the twenty-first century—where the children will believe what they want coming from an inside point of view not what someone else forces upon them. As I have said in my *Rules by Which a Great Empire May Be Reduced,* "We have constitutional liberty, both of person and of conscience" (459).And in today's society, which is most liberal than most and living up the American dream, I don't think that train of thought will travel far.

TP:[1] You know, with all due respect, I feel that it should be left to the students to decide what they will choose. It's not like you really have a choice here. I don't think that students should be pushed either way with religion, but should be open and be able to make their own decisions. As I have written in *Age of Reason,* "I believe the equality of man, and I believe that religious duties consist in doing justice, loving mercy, and endeavoring to make our fellow creatures happy" (643). The doings of good deeds is equally, if not as, important as making room for God. LOL.

JE: Hey, do you think that's funny? Are you mocking religion? How should the students be able to know what is good for them if they have never experienced it? Maybe that's why you were not with me for the first while up here!

TP: Hold your tongue. Keep your fingers still! This is not the path to which I was going. I did not mean in any way to insult you but just wanted to be open and let the students do as they please as long as they are not harming anyone.

BF:[2] Let us stop squabbling, and silent be. These students are trying to use their time wisely. Let us learn from their industrious habits. Poor Richard says, "Lost time is never found again; and what we call time enough, always proves little enough" (452). I must commend these students for taking the time out of their busy lives for education. For with education and toil of knowledge brings riches and earned results from the combination of the two. "Sloth, by bringing on diseases, absolutely shortens life" (452). The students toil through distraction and trouble to prevent continuous rubble.

JE:[2] Alright with your poetry already. You portray it as if these children will be to heaven directly sent. Damn doeth call to those who turn a head and cheek from the bible urn. "But surely they have no interest in the promises of the covenant of grace who are not the children of the covenant, who do not believe in any of the promises, and have no interest in the Mediator of the covenant" (429).

TP:[2] With all due respect, I request to differ. "I offer nothing more than...plain arguments, and common sense" (631).Through the education of science, the children will be obtaining a closeness to god. "It is a fraud... to call the sciences human inventions" (646). The starry heavens are visible "to teach him science and the arts" (648). These students at Hudson Valley will experience a spirituality never attained prior to their knowledge of the sciences learned here. This is one of the reasons I am following this class and its discussions. The students really open up to this new information and internalize it to better their lives and realize that there is a greater being out there.

JE: How dare you type such preposterous, outlandish thoughts? Where are your brains?

BF: Jonathan, you need to calm down. Keep your temperance in check. Read not to dullness, communicate not to elevation. Allow your innards to calm your heat, "Avoiding trifling conversation" (526). "Let all your things have their places. Let each part of your business have its time" (526). Jonathan, if this conversation is too much for you to handle presently, you may resolute to "perform what you ought" and either leave this chat room or "cut off all unnecessary actions" (526).

TP:[3] These students are the future. They will go out into the world and prove that there can exist a harmony developed from the cornerstones of the mind, into fortresses of safe and solid communities. For I believe that this is the purpose of science: to open up the eyes of man and behold the beauty that He has created. "Nothing was made in vain; for in vain would be this power of vision if it taught man nothing" (649).

JE:[3] I will have to agree with you on the point that these will be the leaders of tomorrow. However, my missionaries are doing their work well. They will forge ahead with opening up the eyes of blind students to the faith and all will end well in heaven, for "Whoever sinneth, hath not seen him, nor known him" (411). "And this is eternal life, that they might know thee" (411).

BF:[3] I am not so hot with you on that point, but if I may add—"'Tis hard for an empty bag to stand upright" (456). You know, poverty "often deprives a man of all spirit and virtue" (456). I therefore believe that these forgers will go ahead into the future with a degree and financial success under their belt. This will help keep the American dream alive. "Disdain the chain, preserve your freedom; and maintain your independency: be industrious and free; be frugal and free. At present, perhaps, you may think yourself in thriving circumstances, and that you can bear a little extravagance without injury; but, 'For age and want, save while you may; No morning sun lasts a whole day'" (456).

TP: Wow. You almost sound like you are giving them their graduation lecture. Has it not just been midterms?

JE: Yes, and may I call your attention to the beginning of this conversation. This is a project due on Monday the first of November. I look forward to reading responses, and I am curious to know how many hold religion as a pivotal role in their lives and decision making in today's age.

TP: And I as well. Curious to see which students portray the strength with which to stand up for themselves today, for this will be a reflection for tomorrow.

BF: I think I will find it interesting to see which students put thought into this project. Who will be "employ'd in something useful. Cut off all unnecessary actions" (526).

JE: My angels are calling. GTG. Good night.

TP: Ben?

BF: Yes.

TP: Sorry for losing my cool, but his religious excitement presses my turn off button.

BF: I understand Tom. You might want to deliberate your swift loss of patience and work on it so that next time the conversation will steer clear of friction.

TP: You carry a good point. Have a restful night.

BF: Good night.

---

[i] WTF = Whatever They Figure

[1] The view of these characters in reference to religion in the twenty-first century (and specifically with regards to Hudson Valley Community College students).

[2] The point of view of each of the chosen characters with regards to the industriousness and direction of students in the twenty-first century.

[3] The views and predictions of the characters chosen with regards to the future of America and its direction begins here—with the students at HVCC.

The "N" Word

Tanisha Cromwell

Growing up as a modern day African American in urban America, I have been exposed to an array of names that are used to describe or identify myself as a black person. However, I have never seen a word as controversial and highly debated word as the word "nigga." What is the debate about it? Black leaders want the word banned because of its historical meaning and how it was used to degrade and belittle blacks. However, today, the word isn't used in the same context but in a more positive way.

First, let me say that the spelling is different. I would say pre-Civil Rights Movement, the word was spelled "nigger" and it was used to describe African Americans. There are many explanations behind the origin of the word. One is that is derived from the Latin word *nigrum,* which is black. Another explanation behind the origin of the word is that White people used the word to describe where the Africans came from, which was near the Niger River, thus referring to the Africans as niggers. Despite where the word may have derived from, it was not used in a polite or respectable manner.

Post-Civil Rights Movement, and during the Black Panther Movement, the word's pronunciation and spelling changed to what we know now as *nigga.* This variation of the word is the one that is highly criticized because the word that was once so disrespectful to Blacks is now being used by African Americans themselves as a term of endearment. They figured that changing the spelling of the word and removing its context would drain out the negativity that the word once had and change it to something positive.

Nigga has been used since then. It has been integrated into our everyday lives as we hear it in hip-hop lyrics, in movies and even in many comedians' stand-up routines. Comedian Richard Pryor used the word so often in his acts that he even named one of his stand-ups "That Nigger's Crazy." A legendary hip-hop act from California was named N.W.A., or Niggas Wit Attitude. The late and legendary rapper Tupac Shakur often used the word in titles of his songs. He also gave his input on the word. He said, "Niggers was the ones on the ropes, hanging off of things. Niggas is the ones with gold ropes, hanging out in the club." Tupac went as far as to make "nigga" an acronym for "Never Ignorant; Getting Goals Accomplished."

This didn't sit well with everyone. On July 7, 2007, the National Association for the Advancement of Colored People (NAACP), which has been a longtime proponent for the civil rights of African Americans, along with Kwame Kilpatrick, who was the Mayor of Detroit at that time, and the Revs. Jesse Jackson and Al Sharpton held a "funeral" in Detroit, Michigan, for the word "nigger" and its other variations. They felt that "nigga" still had the negative undertone despite its use in a more positive light. The Revs. Jackson and Sharpton have as much as challenged rappers and the newer generation of comedians to stop using the word overall. Old school comedian Bill Cosby even expressed his disgust over the word and over the younger generations' constant use of it in their everyday vocabulary.

I, for one, see nothing wrong with the word nigga because, to me, it no longer has that disrespectful undertone that it once had. I refer to myself as a nigga because it is my way of identifying with a group of people. The meaning of the word nigga has changed since first being introduced in the English language, but for the better.

Nigga is a word that has been embedded in the minds of the African American youth, and the word is here to stay.

Deployment

Carol Walkley

I thought
With you gone life would be unbearable.
It was. Until the routine kicked in.
And you were.
You have nothing but what you carry
Body weight on your back
Alice Pack.
Your pictures of us already torn and faded.
Yet I still complain
How the PX has no jeans, the kids have runny noses, the air
conditioner is broken,
And it is 85 degrees.
Woe is me.
You never have complained, covered always in fine sand,
Eating a peck with every MRE,
Only saying you wish you were here to take the stress
Off my shoulders.
Woe is me?
I cannot give up all of my creature comforts.
We must bathe and eat
Shop and play.
But
I stripped the bed we share,
Saved the sand unintentionally sent in all your letters,
Dug out my old girl scout sleeping bag,
And sleep like you,
Always with you.

"Catbird," by Hannah Bewsher

"Spring Showers," by Abby Gilbert

"Chomp," by Vicki Bower

"Stone," by Hannah Bewsher

In the Space

Heinz Granderath

"Granderath, get up it's time for watch."It was about six in the morning and I just reported to my ship a few hours before. I was given a pair of steamers and told to "hit the pit." This was it, I was about to encounter my very first watch on the USS Frank Cable AS-40. Groggily rolling out of my rack, I dressed out and headed to the Engine Room. I wasn't too sure of what to expect so I put in my earplugs, opened the access door, and headed down the ladder well. The intense heat rushed upon me and I felt as if I couldn't breathe. When I finally reached the bottom of the access, I hadn't a clue what I should do. None of the other watch standers even looked at me. When they finally did, it was with a kind of "Who the fuck is this guy?" look. I knew no one, and I was far from home—ten thousand miles to be exact. I was the new guy and it was time to start paying my dues. Within ten minutes I was drenched in my own sweat, and I hadn't even done any work yet.

Walking through the industrial maze was initially intimidating. I had only read about the equipment and now that I was actually seeing it, the books seemed like they must have been written in Chinese. Seeing the real thing captivated me. On the Engine Room upper level there were massive pieces of machinery dwarfing me. I was engulfed in noises I had never heard. The clunks, clanks, booms, and bangs were too much to take in at once. My alarm clock seemed soothing at this point. Everything was shaking and had its own noise. It was like an orchestra of monsters. There were the distilling plants that turned sea water into potable water. Electrical switchboards that seemed like they came out of a mad scientists laboratory. The turbine generators with their stream drains and immense heat all located in such a close proximity made me imagine what it felt like to be on the sun. In front was the throttle board and main control, which was where the top watch standers were. There were too many gauges to count, and it wasn't the place to be caught standing around.

As I made my way to the Engine Room lower level, I was reminded of my elementary school playground because I had to climb or hang on things just to get around. The worst part was that I had to be careful with everything I touched, for it was usually scalding hot. On one side were the three air conditioning plants, which acted more like the Three Stooges because they never seemed to act normal. In the center of the Engine Room was (but of course), the Main Engine. Comparing the other equipment to the Main Engine was like comparing a gazelle to a lion. Being the king of this jungle, it had quite an ominous roar. This steel god looked like it belonged on the battlefield. Before I could continue exploring I heard over the intercom, "In the space, all nonqualified watch standers lay to the throttle board," and I assumed I would be assigned my first task. What were they going to have me do? Operate this, fix that? I was so excited. Coffee bitch was not my name but it's what I felt like, seeing as that's what I ended up being. I wanted something more and unfortunately I got it.

I cleaned more than I had ever expected to. I didn't know things could get that dirty. The funny thing was they were never even clean when I was done, just less filthy. I didn't really have much of an appetite because I had plenty of dirt to snack on. Cleaning down there was no easy task. The bilge, which is the lowest place possible to go in the Engine Room, was where I was usually assigned to clean along with the rest of the unqualified watch standers. This was the dirtiest of the dirty and where everything and anything fell. It was like a sea of metal snakes. Hundreds of pipes twisting and turning in every direction, which were quite difficult to maneuver around. The wretched smell was nauseating. I had to remove any debris or "gear adrift," as we called it, from the bilge. Everything was considered "gear adrift." Tools and trash were the easy stuff to pick up. However, the concoction of all the materials (dirt, fuel, oil, water, urine, etc...) that fell into the bilge created a thick black sludge that could only be scooped out. This stuff redefined the word disgusting and made me want to vomit. At this point I didn't even have an appetite for dirt anymore. When I was finished, if someone would have shaken my hand, they would have thought I was black. I was allowed to go back to the berthing, shower and hit my rack, only to wake up in six hours and do it again for another six hours, and so on.

Times weren't always easy by any means but eventually, after a few years and excruciatingly hard work, the Machinery Division became my family. Together, we fought, laughed, and sailed around the world. I qualified Throttleman, controlling two enormous steam valves which controlled the Main Engine and speed of the ship. I was basically a human gas and brake pedal. I didn't always have a smile on my face, but I did keep my head held high. The overall, undying pride I take in the things I did with my crew has given me a greater sense of accomplishment. I climbed my way out of the bilge and now I was the one responsible for monitoring all those gauges. I am truly grateful for my experiences in the United States Navy.

Excerpt: Nine-Month Winter

Hannah Bewsher

After three days on the shrinking land bridge, the company of migrating refugees was in poor shape, and the rising sea was showing them little mercy. The horizon was blooming with thunderheads that flashed with pink, acidic lightning. Tessa's bell-like voice cut the tense night.

"Ivan, you'd better come see this." Tessa was standing at the very edge of the water when Ivan appeared from the back of the caravan. The waves broke strangely at her feet as she looked down at what lay there.

The gears were rusted and poked through the rubber skin like broken bones. The mechanical whale was one of the first Synthetic Marine Mammals (S.M.M.s) that had been built and introduced to the sea after the creatures in whose image they were created had vanished.

Ivan had seen them before, swimming along their ancient preprogrammed migrations, travelling to breeding grounds, but never breeding, seeking out nursery harbors, or giving birth. Though, even Ivan had never seen a SMM so old or huge.

"The date should be on the skull," Ivan said, as he gestured for Tessa to approach the SMM She glanced back at him hotly. "Just pull the skin back and read what it says," he replied. The woman approached the broken machine as if it was a rancid corpse, only because she had been warned of Synthetic Mammals (SMs) and their ferocious programming, and of how you might assume a creature is broken, and yet it may still bite, or electrocute...

The woman prodded it with her foot first, and when the giant head did not move, nor the optical sensors react, she bent over it and cut a slit in the thick rubber skin on the forehead. She wiggled her fingers in and tore it right down to the nose. Now almost four feet from her first incision, she squinted at the steel skull-plate.

"Synthetic Mammal: Marine, Whale, Northern Right," Tessa looked back at Ivan. He nodded for her to continue. The woman tore a little bit more of the rubberized skin and continued:

"Model 344-99-23. Pod 325. Property of the World Wildlife Replication Fund 2098…" Tessa stood up, looking amazed. "2098…?" She said again, looking down at the whole SM in amazement. Its heavy tail was still suspended in the choppy water, thirty feet off shore. The old hardware creaked as the flukes rose and fell with incoming waves and moonlight glistened across its back.

"This machine," Ivan finally said, "swam around for over five hundred years after the WWRF gave up on the project…" The entire caravan looked at the machine quietly. The constant sound of the waves rushed up and filled the thoughtful silence, as if that silence was a small hole dug in the sand...

This machine was from another time, before the world gave up on preserving fragments of nature. Now humans were a struggling species, and their priorities violently narrowed. The presence of the SMs was an imaginary balance; they couldn't hunt and eat these mechanical animals, though they could make tools and shelter from their bodies.

"Dane! Get up here and see if you can salvage any of this…" Ivan's rough voice brought the Company's attention back to the present.

The young mechanic, Dane, was soon kneeling beside the head of the SM as if praying, but there was no soul to morn. His dark, messy hair fell in his face as he worked. With a sharp twist, the cap on the optical sensor came free in his hand, revealing a complicated circuit board. His initial inspection revealed bad rust and barnacles in the brain; apparently, the machine had been losing its mind for years, and consequently beached itself. The man took a knife and skinned it down to clean, un-diseased parts.

"This is an amazing machine," he said, more to himself than to Ivan. "If I had some time, I would like to try and fix it… but that could take years."

"It will be washed away in a few days," Ivan reminded him.

"I know," Dane said quietly, "I can salvage a lot of this, but how much time it will take and how much we can afford to carry, I don't know…"

"You've got two hours," Ivan said, answering both questions very directly. "I'm sure we can carry whatever you manage to pull out of this thing in that amount of time…"

Dane turned to the rubberized, steel framed carcass to begin harvesting useful parts, when Ivan grabbed his shoulder. Dane turned and looked up at the man carefully. Ivan's tone was very low, so that only they could hear.

"Take whatever you can fashion a weapon out of, Dane…" he said, "We've got another company tailing us."

Dane looked back at the stretch of land that they had covered since they left the mainland, and he saw it; the dark smudge of another caravan grinding along. Dane looked up at Ivan quizzically, his youthful face rosy in the cold.

"You think they would attack us?"

"They could be a little more desperate than us…" Ivan said, squinting over his shoulder. "Or," he added, "We could be a little more desperate than them…" Ivan struck a match and lit the crooked cigarette in his lips, while Dane watched him angrily.

"We aren't pirates, Ivan…"

"We are what we have to be," the man replied coldly, smoke wreathing his face. Dane could not argue with this truth, and he numbly set about his work.

Two hours passed quickly with the sea droning all around him. Dane picked up the huge glass eye again and looked at it closely, rotating it on his fingers. The holographic pupil still flickered in the light, but the surface of the lens was foggy, blind, with scratches.

"Find anything interesting?"

Tessa squatted beside Dane, looking over his shoulder curiously. "Yes, copper," he said, waving a hand at the pile of pipes, wires, and replicated Terylene baleen. "I haven't seen copper in years…"

Caged Animal

Courtney Benson

As I lie in my warm, comfortable bed, I begin to open my eyes. I continue to see darkness. My darkness never gets bright or blurry or even changes in the slightest way. I have seen this darkness for as long as I can remember. Without delay, I stand up, and my arm expands to its fullest length until I find the wall. I begin to walk, my hand always feeling for the wall. Suddenly, the wall ends, and the floor underneath my feet change to a hard, cold surface. Now I know I am leaving my bedroom and entering the hallway. I was born blind; therefore, I rely on my hands to tell me my location.

"Good morning Johnny!" I can hear a voice as it walks closer to me until I feel someone grab my hand. They are leading me to start my day. While the helping hand walks one step ahead of me, I keep my hand stretched out to feel the wall. When I feel the surface of the wallpaper change, I know my favorite chair in the living room is only three steps away. I sit in the chair as I start to analyze different voices that I hear. Most of them sound familiar as soon as I begin to separate one from another. These same voices I have heard for nearly ten years, and these are my housemates. The other voices I hear are less familiar but still comforting, calm, and unperturbed. These tranquil voices are my staff who help me with my everyday living tasks. I feel safe now. Regrettably, my life has not always been this good.

About thirty years ago, all of the staff who worked with me were brutally mean. In 1975, I lived in an institution, not a home. It was a place called Willowbrook State School in Staten Island, New York. It was a state-funded school for men and women of all ages who were born with mental retardation. The memories of my life at Willowbrook will remain with me forever. No person should ever have to live like I did, like a caged animal at a zoo.

It is hard to forget the smell, the sounds, and the conditions I was forced to live in. Many would describe the smell as nauseating or disgusting. I, on the other hand, was used to smell of disease and death that surrounded me. My ears were constantly ringing with the sounds of people crying or yelling or moaning. My fellow "students" were only crying for help. The facility was built to house about 4,500 people, but I lived with over 6,000. The staff who took care of me was very overwhelmed, barely having enough time to keep the place clean. Each staff person had about sixty or seventy developmentally disabled persons to care for. When we were given our meals, comparable to slop, we had to eat fast. I learned very soon that if I would not consume my entire plate in two minutes, someone else would steal it from me. I had to eat with my hands as I was never taught to use silverware. I was starving. My clothes were filthy and soiled with urine most of the time. I wasn't able simply to walk to the bathroom. I had no choice but to relieve myself where I sat, and that is all I did from day to day, just sit in one spot. I could feel the others around me rocking back and forth. I soon learned they were just as bored as I was. No one would ever talk to me. I began repeating, out loud, what words I could make out. It was my only form of entertainment or social interaction.

Willowbrook finally closed its doors in the late 1980s. Over the next 10 years, I was shuffled from group home to group home. My living conditions improved each time. My first real hot shower felt I was being reborn. I was given clean clothes. I was taught how to properly use the bathroom. The meals I ate with silverware were of quality. In 1995, I was able to move into my current home where I am living a "normal life" as a human being.

Mothers Keep Secrets Too

Erika Davis

There was a time in my life where I completely loathed my mother, particularly throughout junior and senior year of high school. She was constantly telling me what to do, preventing me from staying out late with my friends, and relentlessly apprehending me for everything I did. During this time, I was also incredibly disrespectful, self-absorbed, and unappreciative toward her and the unconditional love and support she presented me with on a daily basis. That was until one day, one day I will never forget.

I needed to apply for a passport, and to do so, a copy of my birth certificate was required. My mother sent me into the dungeon, also known as the basement. There is a shiny, black, fireproof safe where my parents keep an array of important documents and personal information tucked inside. I began to rifle through years of paperwork in search of the folder labeled, "Birth Certificates and Social Security Cards." Instead, I found a disassembled, yellowed and crinkly, spiral-bound notebook. I felt guilty reading what was inside, but it was just what I needed to realize everything my mother had sacrificed for me, and how truly lucky I was.

It was not a real diary by any means. It was more a collection of notes, lists, and thoughts. At times she would write consecutively, and other times multiple days would pass before something was jotted down. I knew there was something personal about the notebook, but I snooped anyway. There was an entry written shortly after I was born, when my mom had taken some time off from work to take care of me. Because she was not working, money was tight. She wrote about how my father would give her twenty dollars per week for spending money. As I continued reading, I learned that diapers for the week cost twelve dollars, leaving eight dollars to ration between food for her and everything else I needed. Apparently when she asked for more, my father would give her a hard time, and she continually mentioned how, "It wasn't worth the battle." My stomach began to curl as I was trying to imagine getting by with twenty dollars per week for myself. I could not imagine taking care of myself on that kind of income, nonetheless trying to care for an infant as well. Suddenly, I felt selfish. Part of me wanted to stop, but I kept reading.

Around the same time frame, my mom stressed how much she wanted to go back to work, simply because she was poor. When she suggested it in conversation to my father, he refused to let her return to work, for then they would have to pay a babysitter. She proceeded to mention topics of their conversation, mostly concerning money. Later that evening, she asked him for money to buy underwear. Apparently, the few pairs she did have were beginning to resemble Swiss cheese, barely hanging together from hole to tear. I had high hopes for my father at the end of this entry, but I remained disappointed.

The last entry I began reading nearly brought tears to my eyes. I shut the notebook not even halfway through the scribbled thoughts and threw it back in the safe. Never in my wildest dreams had I thought anything of the kind of sacrifices and hardships she went through. She never once mentioned anything about an unfortunate past, financial issues, or troubles between my father and her. She was always telling me, "You should be thankful for what you have, and remember that someone always has it worse." I never really understood what that advice meant until I came across that notebook.

I ran upstairs with my birth certificate and placed it on the counter. I walked to where my mother was standing and told her that I love her and that I appreciate everything she does for me. From then on, our relationship was different, but it was better. It is amazing how easy it is to take advantage of so many things in this world. My mother has worked forty-plus hour weeks for as long as I can remember, meanwhile maintaining a three-bedroom home with a sizable backyard. She has also managed to ensure that my siblings and I got everything we needed, and some of what we wanted. I never thanked her enough or showed her the respect she deserved, but now, I do just that, every day.

An Overview of Haiti

Kim Belizaire

Port-au-Prince, the capital of Haiti is a city with a high crime rate. In Port-au Prince the police is corrupt, the different political gangs are the ones in power, and there are great amount guns available to the general public.

In Port-au-Prince, to join the police force having a high school diploma is not even one of the requirements. And colleges are so expensive that asking a candidate to have a college degree would probably be considered a crime. In addition, the government does not provide any form of help to encourage students to pursue a college level education. A police officer does not get paid a lot of money and considering the fact that they have to support their family and themselves, taking bribes is one of the common ways of adding the missing dollars to their salary. Another problem with the police officers are that they are always using their power to abuse the population and take revenge for a family member and themselves.

The political parties are not like the common parties around the world. Instead, their leaders are heavy drug users who just want to be part of the government so they can do all the illegal stuff without being asked any questions. People who are part of the political system are usually not educated because the government is corrupt. And a diploma can be provided to anybody in any field of study, for the right price. Political gangs are a big part of the system, and when they are not popular enough to win the elections, a candidate can actually buy the election, just for the right price.

Gun availability is also a major problem in Port-au-Prince. Illegal guns are going back and forth, in and out of the city. There are also all types of guns. Sometimes the civilians have more powerful weapons than the police and that's why they usually get scared and take bribes. Teenagers, who are probably the most irresponsible human beings, are also gun owners. They formed their own gangs and fight each other. Once, on television, the media showed a fourteen year old who was the owner of fifty illegal guns. The Constitution is full of laws about the criteria for someone to be a gun owner, but these laws are not respected by anyone.

Port-au-Prince, the capital of Haiti, is a city with a high crime rate, where money can buy you anything from a high school diploma to an election. Illegal guns are also another problem for the city, but the government is not willing to help because it would include losing their power and their ability to use the country to get rich and to corrupt.

To Men Who Rule the World

Candace Perry

To Men Who Rule the World,

I just want to first and foremost applaud you; in fact I will give you a standing ovation. I will stand up, clap my hands and stomp my feet, whistle, hoot, and cheer for you.

I will stand there proud with a look upon my face of someone who is there to show moral support, be understanding and finally to congratulate you. I will congratulate you, for being the greatest guy in the world. The one who everyone looks up to and wants to become, the one who is intelligent, loving, and compassionate. You care about others and their feelings, taking into consideration that everyone is emotionally different and they too need to express themselves.

Shall I continue praising you, stroking your ego while you gloat thinking to yourself how you deluded those around you. You chuckle to yourself for pulling wool over everyone's eyes and think to yourself how moronic everyone around you is for not truly distinguishing how deceptive you have truly been.

I want to thank you for allowing me and others to get a glimpse of your other side, your other side that you have kept hidden so well. Thank you for allowing us to see the true you, the two-faced person that you truly are.

This letter is addressed to you egotistical, selfish, impudent, ignorant men who think that the world revolves around you. You feel like you are a man by putting others down, degrading woman, referring to them as your property. You treat woman as if they are nothing and you want them to be docile, passive, and submissive.

You are callous, misleading, and fraudulent; you put on an act for everyone else, acting as if you are this great person but really you are a monster. You put people down to build yourself up, you are never satisfied, and nothing makes you happy.

You look for reasons to argue, reasons to fight. You start by making a comment or questioning something that she has done. You then wait for a response—a response that you didn't want. You didn't want a response at all, you wanted to hear nothing because to you that is back-talking, and how dare she back-talk you. Yet if she didn't say anything at all you'd then start to argue about that because you'd think she was ignoring you. Either way she was doomed, she knew it and you knew it too. It was a trick question where every answer was wrong. To you it was a just game; to her it was her means of survival. She knew what was bound to happen for it happens frequently and as much as she tries to derail and stall the inevitable, she cannot. She can only wait and remain helpless for this dark, cold, monster to strike. While you see what she is trying to do, you smirk and watch her squirm for you get nothing but gratification by doing so. When you are done toying with her like a cat would a mouse you eventually pounce striking her with your balled fists one after another. She screeches, cries, and pleads with you to stop yet you don't. She knows not to fight back because it will only anger you further so she does the only thing she can do and that is to ball up and cover her face and head to keep from blacking out but also to keep from getting any bruises where they will be seen by others. She then waits while you continue to attack her body, taking all your anger and frustration out on her as if she is a punching bag. She is shaking and crying, and she wonders why you are doing this and what she has done this to time to anger you. Finally, after you're satisfied with the damage you have done, you stand over her and stare, saying nothing. You stand and wait, wait for her to say something, wait for her to move. She knows the routine: You are putting her through another one of your rigorous tests, and if she fails, the consequences will be dire. She does nothing, yet for some reason you choose to become enraged because of this and kick her a few times, followed by a mouth full of degrading name calling, telling her that she is worthless, fat, and ugly and how no one will ever want her or love her. You finish her off by doing the most degrading thing there is to do, you spit on her as if you are disgusted with her, and she is nothing more than trash. You then walk off saying nothing, returning to what you were doing as if this never happened.

I would say that someone should do the same to you, punch you like a punching bag, and then throw you away like the trash that you are. But you know what I've got something better than that, and you want to know what that is?

You being exposed. You being exposed as nothing more and nothing less than the woman abuser that you are. I know that in the end this will hurt you more than you physically being hurt would, because you being exposed means you being stripped of your dignity.

She may have to endure your abuse but one day she will be set free; however, you won't. You will be titled a woman abuser, and you will have to carry that with you forever. You will forever be titled, tainted, and branded. That alone is equivalent to being abused day in and day out. Now you can see what it's like and how it feels to be treated like dirt.

Now that you have been exposed, I wish you all the best in your life of hell. Rot slowly, and enjoy having a pathetic, torturous, life.

Sincerely,
Candace Perry
#1 Fan of Hoping-You'll-Be-the-First-to-Drop-Dead Fan Club

Bought and Sold

Anthony Cochetti

The rain splashed underneath the tires of the vehicle, a path riven through the tumultuous pools of water. I drove slowly through the narrow street, eyeing the people who walked on either side. My headlights did little to pierce the wall that poured around me and the people moved as though a strobe passed over them, one moment invisible and the next frozen by the brief view granted by the rain. I exhaled, painting the windshield with my breath. My heater was broken.

After a few minutes I turned the car onto a side street and parked in front of a bar. A dim yellow glow passed through the windows almost opaque with dirt. A malfunctioning neon sign indicated that the business was open. Above the door was the name of the place, "Murphy's."

I removed the key from the ignition and opened the door, immediately unfurling an umbrella and sparing the seat of the car the worst of the rain. I closed and locked the car and walked around to the door of the bar. Trying the handle, the door opened with a creak that was barely heard over the din of the inebriated. It was just four in the afternoon but people had no eyes for the time in this part of town, only eyes for a pint of beer. The talk stopped as soon as I stepped in. They looked at me in a stupor edged with malice. Drunken malcontents that didn't appreciate the interruption.

As I walked across the room toward the bar, a few forgot me and returned to their drinks. The bartender stared at me, idly wiping a glass with a grayed rag he likely used the day before.

He wasn't terribly fat but I wouldn't bet on him in a race. He wore a vest and was balding, living up to the stereotype.

"What do you want?" he asked me. I sat down at the bar in front of him and stowed my umbrella underneath the stool.

"Some information," I told him. "I'm looking for someone." He pressed his lips in a grim line.

"I haven't got a damn thing to say to some self-sold dog," he told me. I began to get the feeling that he didn't appreciate the services of a private eye. I laid my hand on the table and left a hundred in front of him.

"There's more for your cooperation. My client is very interested in my success." He nervously eyed the bill; the conflict was clear on his face, but he made his decision quickly enough. He looked at me and nodded to the back of the bar.

"Leave out the front and come around back. I'm not gonna have somebody seeing you."

I came down off of my stool and reached down for my umbrella but it was gone. Nicked while I was paying attention to the bartender. It didn't matter, I wasn't about to pull it out of this crowd at any rate. I left with the bar's eyes on my back.

Back outside in the rain I turned the corner and walked into the alley. It was full of soaking wet garbage, the bags ripped open by cats or raccoons. I turned to edge past it toward the bar's side door. It opened for me and I was led into what looked like the bartender's office. Reams of ribbon paper covered the desk, a cash box was surrounded by stacks of money and rolls of change. The bartender sat in a chair that had bent to fit his shape. This whole sad scene was lit by a yellowing lamp on top of a paper stack.

"So talk," I prodded him.

"Money first," he returned. I shrugged and dug in my pocket for another hundred. I tossed it down on the desk with the rest of his take. He took the bill and held it to the light, checking it.

Satisfied, he laid it back down on the desk. He looked up then, past me. I tried to turn around but a gun pressed against my neck stopped me cold.

The bartender smiled for the first time but I wish he hadn't. His teeth matched the whiskey he sold out front.

"Who did you think you were fooling coming out here?" he asked, amused. "You think we wouldn't know they'd send someone for the girl? Your boss is going to have to dig a little deeper next time and buy a pup that doesn't blunder into the hornet's nest." I stayed shut up and kept a neutral expression on my face.

"Don't get me wrong, we're so glad to have you here. We were wondering how to explain the situation to your guy. You'll do nicely." The bartender nodded to the guy behind me. The gun slammed into the side of my head, nearly knocking me out of the chair. Pain detonated inside of my head and fought for my attention, pushing everything else back. I felt myself being pulled straight. The bartender was speaking again.

"Don't worry about your head, there, you won't need it."

Another vicious shot at my head knocked me over, the chair landing on top of me. I pulled myself out from underneath and was rewarded with a kick in the chest, knocking the wind out of me. I wrapped my arms around myself and tried to force air into my lungs. The nails in the floor boards danced in front of my eyes with ghostly partners. I filled my lungs and coughed, finishing in time to hear the gun.

Favorite Song

Nicholas Buonanno

It was a warm sunny day in May of 2010, my best friend Michael and I were driving around in my new car. I had just bought a 2007 Mitsubishi Eclipse. We were just driving around talking and playing the music that was on the CD that I made. The song that was playing was "Airplanes" by B.O.B. At the time I didn't really think too much of the song for some kind of meaning, I just thought it was a good song.

A few days later Michael called me to ask what the name of that song was, and then I noticed that he started playing that song a lot. I thought that it must have reminded him of the carefree feeling we had felt that day in my car.

A few weeks later, I realized why he really liked this song so much. I had found out that my best friend had only three more weeks to live. He had leukemia and was only eighteen. The first day he was diagnosed with cancer was in the eighth grade. Throughout the five years of him battling this illness I would make sure I would always be there for him. I would go visit him all the time in the hospital and whenever we would hang out we would just talk about regular teenage stuff. I never wanted to talk with him about the cancer, I just wanted him to have a fun time and not have to worry about it all the time.

Now I love to listen to this song in honor of him and I always think of him while listening. The part of the song that has the most meaning is when they say, "Can we pretend that airplanes in the night sky are like shooting starts? I can really use a wish right now." This whole time he wanted that wish to be able to live longer and fight this disease. This song has had such an impact on me, after everything that has happened. I ended up getting three shooting stars tattooed on me, so I will always remember the day we listened to this song in my car. Now, every day I sit here wishing that he could still be here.

Great Teachers Inspire

Sierra Sturdivant

William Arthur Ward said, "The mediocre teachers tell. The good teacher explains. The superior teacher demonstrates. The great teacher inspires." Teachers have a greater impact on their students than they may believe or care to know. Students are with their teachers more than they're with their friends and family; what students are taught in school, and who they're taught by, may stay with them longer than what a parent says. There are many types of different teachers that can be characterized and classified into multiple categories. Teachers are like a box of chocolates: One is never the same as another, and you never know what's inside until you try it. There are teachers that are fun, boring, nonchalant, always get off subject, give too much information, have their own children or have previously taught children, and many more. At no point in time will all your teachers have the same personalities or ways of teaching.

There is one type of teacher that I've had every year since junior high school; it's always a nonchalant man. When he teaches he seems very laid back, has no worries, and nothing affects him. The only reason he gives tests is because he has to or else there's no other way to see if we've been paying attention. Other than that he would never give exams. He gives assignments that rarely have exact due dates. I had a teacher in high school who would tell us everything that was due and then say hand it in next week. At the beginning of the school year, we would always ask what day, and his exact words were, "Whenever, it doesn't matter." After a while, we obviously caught on and stopped asking. We started out loving him because the class seemed to be a breeze, but then we started to realize that he didn't set deadlines because he figured we wouldn't hand it in anyway. Although this is not true for all nonchalant teachers, I feel like he had no hope in us.

Another type that I've had more than enough times are the teachers who always get off subject; they are like five-year-old children with A.D.D. They don't seem to be able to concentrate long enough to even explain what's on the syllabus for the day. I have a professor now that, in a fifty minute class, only taught fifteen minutes of subject matter. Everything else we sit through in the class is pointless; it will never be presented on a quiz, test, or exam. He takes up thirty-five minutes of class time speaking about his wife and daughter and bragging about the property he owns. To most students, he is the perfect teacher; to me on the other hand, teachers like him are unnecessary. I go to class for clarification; if I'm not getting that, I might as well have taken an online class and taught myself. I feel like I already do this, because if I don't read, I'd never pass his tests due to the fact that he doesn't cover what he needs to during the allotted time.

Too much information after a while is not needed and becomes irritating. Teachers who tell too much on one piece of material are like comedians who tell run-on jokes. The listener at first is interested, ready to hear more, and sitting on the edge of his or her seat. By the time the comedian is finally getting to the punch line, the listener is sitting all the way back, awaiting a conclusion that they know is not going to be worth hearing, and is most likely zoned off into another world. I once had a teacher who, if you asked a question, would first tell you why the question was important or not, how it pertained to her class, repeat the question for everyone to hear, then explain to the class why she thought you asked the question. By the time she said all of that, we didn't even care anymore. If you noticed, not once in the entire process did I say she answered the question. None of what she said helped me at all in her class. I had another teacher, who we referred to as Doctor, due to his level of education. He was one of the smartest men I've ever met. If I ever had a question about anything he would be the person I went to, but only if I had about an hour to spare. I could asked the simplest question that needed a one word answer and he would tell me everything he knew about that specific topic, then answer the question. Though he helped me very much in high school, when did I ever have an hour to spare?

The teachers I look forward to learning from are the ones who have their own children, or have previously taught. To me, they're the best. These types of teachers are more patient than the rest. They are used to answering questions one after another without getting confused or annoyed. Their minds seem to move quicker than other teachers because they're always a step ahead of students. These teachers are the ones that are like parents: caring, nurturing, and helpful—even when you don't ask for it. They lead and guide you down the right path and have no problem with scolding you. I may not like them too much at the beginning of the school year because they never smile and seem to be very strict, but by the time the school year is over, they've loosened up, and I've noticed an improvement in my work. I once had a teacher who would call my house at the beginning of every week to tell my parents every assignment given and when it was going to be due. It wasn't that I didn't do the work; she just said that I didn't do them to the best of my ability. My mom told her at open house, if there was anything she needed, to contact her, and my teacher definitely took advantage of that offer. I was grateful to her, and my parents were as well. My grade went from a C to an A within one quarter. This is the type of teacher I wish I could have every school year; one that sees your potential and makes you act on it.

Everyone has a different opinion about teachers and the way they teach. My experiences support my theory. Students like teachers for multiple reasons. A student may like a teacher because he or she thinks the teacher's class is easy; on the other hand, this could be the exact reason another student dislikes him/her. I personally like teachers that push me. The teacher that inspired me the most was the one that made me think when I didn't want to, speak when I was shy, and write when I had nothing to say. That teacher made me think that I could make it to the top when I had no hope in myself. She made me see the best in me. Ken Blanchard said, "Your role as a leader is even more important than you might imagine. You have the power to help people become winners." The teachers who understand and abide by this quote are the ones whose students excel further than they ever imagined. I now know I was made to win.

My Literacy Timeline

Dan Mancuso

My story begins some twelve years ago. I had successfully completed kindergarten; I played nice and was looking forward to first grade. It was at this time that my mother was discovering teaching, but she wanted to look before she leaped. So she decided to try it out on her children. I basically skipped first grade; when I should have been in school learning to read and count, I was being "homeschooled." A regular day of classes in the Mancuso household consisted of my mom putting a worksheet in front of me, getting distracted, and then me playing with my toys for the rest of the day. Needless to say that was the only year I was homeschooled, so when I went back for second grade, I had the knowledge of a kindergartener. This included not knowing what came after C in the alphabet.

My mother recognized that I had a problem and, fortunately for me, that she couldn't teach to save her life. But to my good fortune, my great aunt had once been an elementary school teacher. So it was reading lessons at Aunt Mary Myers every Saturday. I don't remember much from the experience, but one event stands out. I was sitting at her table trying to read a book about fire trucks, which was remarkably difficult, when she said, "Okay, that's enough for now. Go get some cookies, and grab a few for me, too!" It caught me off guard seeing as I had read no more than two or three sentences. But this was the way she taught, and it worked fantastically well! Suffice to say, I knew my letters.

I would read anything I could get my hands on, so it was only a matter of time before I began indulging in material that was way out of my league. It was during fifth grade that I plowed through *The Lord of the Rings* for the first time, and the summer before sixth when I first read *Catch-22*. Of course, I had no idea what was going on in these novels but I kept plugging away. I suppose it was because I engaged in such advanced reads that my focus soon changed, I got bored. For the first half of high school, I didn't even touch a full-fledged novel, outside of school of course. I would squander away hours laughing at the stupid knock-knock jokes you find in the pint-sized joke books. If I wasn't doing that I would be skimming through a booklet of facts, you know the type; with tidbits like "If the entire population of China were to walk past you in single file, you would not live long enough to see the end of the line."

Along with my obsession with joke books and miniature factoids was my newly designed "reading period." By this I mean I had taught myself to read only at a certain time of the day. I suppose the reason for this was because I was starting to get really busy with all things teen, and that books filled with facts are only so interesting. At bedtime, I would grab whatever happened to be on my desk, read it for a few minutes, then drift off to sleep. The latest work of literature to find its way to my desk is the Bible, certainly a far cry from a joke book. I suppose my progress would be much faster, but I can't seem to break myself of this habit, reading only in bed. But that's just for now, as for what's to come, who knows? With any luck I'll be reading some more interesting novels, perhaps even in the middle of the day.

Thanks, Mr. Weinlein

Sarah Pfeiffer

This year marks ten years that I have been tromping through life unabashedly stating, "If it wasn't for Mr. Weinlein, I wouldn't have graduated high school."I realize this sounds a little extreme, but by the end of my freshman year, I was fast approaching the family tradition of not graduating.

After a childhood of going through the motions with my mouth shut and my eyes down, I found myself suddenly, and uncontrollably, angry. I skipped classes, hung out with the wrong people, and spent my time getting to know the staff in the principal's office. As you can imagine, the avalanche of so-called "help" ensued: reprimands followed by several meetings with my mom, rounded up with detention, suspension, and counseling. Of course, that simply cemented the idea that I was a bad student who didn't care.

In reality, I was a teenager, struggling through adolescence, and finally reacting to all of the compartmentalized memories and emotions of a highly dysfunctional childhood. Add to that the confusion of being a gay youth in the late nineties, and you've got yourself a kid who can't be helped. That is, until I was introduced to Gregg Weinlein.

In a last ditch effort, I was set up to meet with the director of my school's alternate program. Sitting at the first meeting, slumped, inwardly rolling my eyes, I listened to Mr. Weinlein explain why the alternate program was different. The class sizes were much smaller, the students had classes with only a few teachers who taught multiple subjects, and everyone was there to support each other no matter what. That last part got my attention.

"You mean, if I have a problem I can go to you and talk about it even if I have to miss a class?" Without hesitation, Mr. Weinlein answered, "Anytime. My door is always open." I felt sure this was some sort of trap and made it my personal mission to expose his clearly fake support.

I was now in classes of ten or twelve peers, rather than the standard twenty or thirty. I experienced teachers who looked you in the eye and didn't let you get away with anything less than your best, even if your best wasn't very good yet. I found myself amidst passionate debates that sometimes exploded in the middle of a lecture, and were encouraged to continue. Over time, the feeling amongst the students was that of acceptance, camaraderie, and pride to be a part of something bigger than themselves. Through it all, I watched a single man shoulder the weight of several titles: administrator, teacher, counselor, father figure, and friend. That same man faced opposition, anger, and politics from every angle with a kind heart and a strong conviction. Without knowing it, he taught us to do the same.

Today I sit surrounded by my college textbooks and think of how far I've come in my life. I have a beautiful wife and incredible people filling all areas of my world. I have owned a stained glass business, owned a house, and traveled to Europe. I have experienced extraordinary things, beautiful moments in time that make me ask myself: Would this all be possible if I hadn't graduated high school? The answer that I have found is this: I have the courage and conviction to get to where I'm going no matter what, but it sure doesn't hurt to have a leg up along the way. Thanks, Mr. Weinlein.

Hello Jack

Julianne Ruff

You bang on my door
Late at night
And I want to let you in.

I know I'll end up on the floor
After this fight
But I want to let you in.

The rain, it pours
And it thunders with a fright.
Should I let you in?

You scream, "You whore,"
And a fire in your eyes ignites,
But still I let you in.

Hit after hit, I try to ignore
The fact that you excite.
I'm glad I let you in.

You may score
But I lose tonight.
I shouldn't have let you in.

My body you explore
As I give up the fight.
You could have let yourself in.

* * *

You are what I adore.
You make my soul take flight.
I'll always let you in.

Dad

Adam Layh

I recently asked my son what he thought it meant to be a dad. He responded by confidently telling me that "it means being responsible for your family." I thought this was a very intelligent response, from my eight-year-old genius, and it made me think. Although he was correct, in his simple terms, I knew there was so much more. In reality, being a dad is an unanticipated adventure, a constant lesson, and reminder that experience is something you have just after you need it the most.

There are many important, sometimes critical, things to remember when you're a dad. There is no more painful scrutiny than that of your own children. The example you set for them will set the tone for the rest of their lives. Diligence is crucial when remembering these things because it is the slip-ups that they will remember the most. It is usually easy to know when you have made a mistake because you will hear the inevitable phrase uttered, "Daddy does that," or my personal favorite, "Daddy doesn't make me do that."No pressure here...

My boys say there are "four Bs." These "Bs" help them to make day-to-day, minute-to-minute decisions. When they are confronted with a choice they remember to always be respectful, be responsible, be a learner, and be positive. The repetitive use and application of these "Bs" to life is a wonderful bit of wisdom that should be thought about every day.

The first and most important thing about being a dad is to be respectful. Respect is an important lesson that must be learned very young. Children see everything; they see how I interact with the waitress at a restaurant; they see how I talk to their teacher, the bus driver, and even strangers. Setting the example that everyone deserves dad's respect, and theirs, is vastly important. This will help govern the relationships they have as adults. Showing them that you have respect for them is equally important as this will give them confidence in themselves.

As you can already tell, being responsible is something that my boys already understand but it is because of a little thing called Baseball that this is so. There are a lot of concepts to be learned from playing sports. Many of them have nothing to do with the sport itself. Kids crave structure in their lives, and baseball bursts with it.

In the third year of baseball, the rules begin to evolve and strike-outs become part of the game. This, I must admit, was not something I was prepared for. Striking out sucks! I think it was the first time my youngest really felt like he had failed at anything. His reaction was that he didn't want to play anymore. Our conversation on the drive home, which consisted of me promising him that Derek Jeter strikes out all the time, ended with his realization that he had a responsibility to his team, his coach, and himself to finish the season. This interaction proved to be both an exercise in being positive and being a learner.

Being a learner may seem like a simple phrase and something more suited for an elementary school wall, but it holds true no matter how old you are. For instance, doing homework with my kids is an everyday event. We sit together and do our work. If there is none to be done then we read. Dads have a responsibility to set the example that being a learner never ends.

The hardest part of being a dad is making mistakes. No one wants to screw up, so when you know you made a mistake it can be devastating. Staying positive is as obligatory to being a dad as chivalry is to a knight. When times are challenging, and they often are, phrases like "keep your chin up," "look on the bright side," or even "walk it off" become rally calls. Staying positive and being a learner often go together for a dad when dealing with a problem at hand.

Dads do not have any easy job. Often, life can be as hard as it is rewarding. With some care and devotion, being responsible, being respectful, being a learner, and being positive, a dad can overcome all of life's challenges. In all, being a dad is an amazing gift of knowledge that may only be obtained with unwavering patience and constant practice.

The Marine Corp's Backbone: The Four Types of Lance Corporals

Nicholas Anthony Monte

The Boot, the Motivator, The Salt Dog, and the Skater—the average person doesn't know these terms. To the Lance Corporal though, these terms are known all too well. The Lance Corporal is the pay grade E-3 (the third lowest rank) in the United States Marine Corps (USMC). This is the most common rank in the Marine Corps and makes up most of the roster in an infantry platoon. If a civilian were to go to the barracks on Camp Lejeune, they would see many Lance Corporals, and to them they would just be Marines. To an experienced eye though, these four groups of Lance Corporals could be spotted fairly easily.

So you've made it through the Marine Corp's boot camp. You've done two months of the exhausting school of infantry, and now you've made it to the fleet Marine Corp as a new Lance Corporal; so what now? Well you're a Boot, and it won't be long before you know it. The name Boot is given simply because the marine is fresh out of boot camp. To imagine what a Boot looks like on his first day in the fleet, imagine a puppy, lost and waiting for his master to latch his lease back on. The Boot is the most special of all the groups; this is because the other three types of Lance Corporals can mesh, but not the Boot. The Boot is nothing but a boot, and is he is often reminded of it. The Boot is the same rank as the other groups of Lance Corporals, but he is the lowest class of Marine. This somehow forces the Boot to perform slave-like tasks for the other Marines. A few things a Boot often hears are: "Hey Boot, give me a cigarette"; "Clean that up boot face"; "What the

Hell, Boot"; and what he dreads the most, "Working party up." The Boot is the one always sent to do manual labor at what Marines call "working parties," which he soon finds out aren't parties at all. The Boot is usually the most physically fit Lance Corporal. This is only because the Motivator is always forcing workouts with the Boot, simply because he is a Boot. Also the Boot is always running; through fear and reason, the Boot feels the need to run everywhere. This is a common source of entertainment for the other Lance Corporals. Many times I have seen a Boot running across the quad when another Lance Corporal screams, "Get off the grass, Boot," so he runs on the pavement, just to hear a different marine scream, "Get off my pavement, Boot." This will go on until the Boot passes, or until the other Lance Corporals are satisfied. The Boot is usually such a Boot that he can even be picked out in town. He will be in normal clothing but is extremely obvious with his screaming high and tight haircut, Marine Corps t-shirt, and often his Marine Corps backpack. The Boot's time does eventually run out; shortly after the Boot's first deployment is over and he returns home, he is no longer a Boot. At this time, he becomes a Motivator, Skater, Salt Dog, or a combination of two of the three.

I do not mean to say a Boot cannot become a combination of all three classes of Lance Corporal, because a Motivator can be a Salt Dog but never a Skater. In some ways, the Motivator is still like a Boot. He still rocks his high and tight haircut; he will wear unit-specified Marine Corp shirts and is still kind of lost in the sauce. The Motivator is often like a pit bull, constantly barking madly, but no one ever knows why. He is usually the one who is found yelling at or hazing Boots. This is because he truly enjoys it and is always seeking a chance to suck up to the higher ranks. I have often gone into the company office to find at least one Motivator. He can be easily spotted as the dreamy-eyed Marine, taking in every word of his higher ranking Motivators. This usually results in the Motivator picking up the next rank, which is why the Motivator is the shortest-lived type of Lance Corporal. He is also usually disliked by most other Lance Corporals. This being somewhat because of his natural do-gooder attitude, but mostly because of his plans to commit to the unthinkable: to reenlist. Reenlist is a taboo word among most Lance Corporals, an idea that would never cross the mind of a Skater. Reenlistment keeps a Marine around for at least another four years, which is why the Motivator usually becomes a Salt Dog.

The Salt Dog is the most recognizable of the types of Lance Corporals. You have seen him in any war movie. He is usually the one with battle scars, puffing on a big cigar. The Salt Dog could be described as the old battle-ridden pit bull—the one that no other pit bull wants to mess with. This category of Marine comes with the experience of either one but usually two combat deployments. The Salt Dog could be a former or current Motivator, but that is not always the case. He is usually seen leaning up against the barracks smoking a cigarette and smirking, as the Motivators yell at Boots. The Salt Dog can be easily spotted at uniform inspections. He will usually show up late, with a disheveled uniform, but will have a very large stack of ribbons/medals. The Salt Dog is often a well-liked Lance Corporal, and if not, a Motivator will usually be laid-back. He can often be found with a large Gatorade bottle full of dip spit, with a crowd of Boots sitting around him like school children, eager to hear all of his war stories. He at times will hold a lower billet than that of a Motivator, but a Motivator would never test him. The Salt Dog is the embodiment of a Marine Lance Corporal. In most cases, if he is not a reenlisting Motivator, he will turn into the final subcategory of Lance Corporal: the Skater.

The Skater is the most frowned upon type of Lance Corporal there is. All types and ranks of Marine usually disapprove of the Skater, but all envy him in one way or another. The Skater can be described like the small but fast dog. He is hard to find and can duck and weave his master to escape with ease. The Skater is at most times also a Salt Dog or soon to be one. Under no exception is a Skater ever a Motivator, and certainly no Boot can hold the title. The Skater can often not be found; this is the signature of a true Skater. If you were to look at a barracks, you would see a Boot running by, while the Motivator yells and the Salt Dog watches; meanwhile the Skater is in civilian clothes heading to his car for a day at the beach. A common day of a Skater would involve: getting up for formation but only for a minute, then going back to sleep until he awakes sometime around lunch, after lunch maybe some call of duty, then he will self-proclaim himself off work. He manages this through a series of false appointments and possibly a limited duty chit (a doctor's instruction for a marine to do no physical tasks) prescribed for medical reasons. The Skater generally becomes a Skater because he is about to get out of the USMC and simply doesn't care to try anymore, or he is a one-deployment Skater and he never cared in the first place. The Skater never picks up the higher rank and, because of this, is given several nicknames. These include but are not limited to: Lance Cooley, Lance Criminal, and finally, the famed Terminal Lance.

The Boot, the Motivator, the Salt Dog, and the Skater all someday have potential to become a Terminal Lance. This is because a Terminal Lance is not at all a category of a Lance Corporal but a conclusion of one. Becoming a Terminal Lance is at the highest peak of all Lance Corporals. It can only be achieved after four years of active duty in the USMC, and you take your terminal (final) leave up to your last day of active duty. Though you go on terminal leave, you are still and forever a Lance Corporal. I am a Terminal Lance.

In a Drawer

Robert LaSure

A toy gun,
Something, I thought lost,
Along with my childhood,
Memories.

A Celtic rosary,
Aged, as I have,
Something once so dear,
Now, just a trinket.

And a knife.
As sharp as I'm alive.
My reflection,
On its inexperienced blade.

American Psychosis

Chad Coumbes

In recent times, Americans have seen what abused credit lines, racked up debt, and an irresponsible attitude will do to the economy. We live in a consumerist society, where it is the norm to purchase nonessentials in order to promote an image of self-worth. This mentality has directly affected both the economy and social behavior in America.

I was born in the late 1980s. So, growing up in the 1990s, I had direct insight into the behavior of Americans, with regard to financial responsibility. More specifically, I encountered domestic decisions that directly affected me. My mother would be in charge of allocating the family income to pay bills and the like. Often times, she would use some of this money to make purchases for either herself or others. What was the problem with that? She surely saw nothing wrong. However, this would turn out to be a slow building issue, much like a poison, in that it will eventually become glaringly clear that something was amiss. Many Americans made similar decisions with their money, though in some cases on a much larger scale.

After a while, my mother would struggle to juggle bills, while still purchasing non-necessities. My mother had a problem. She felt it necessary to buy in excess to keep up with others, which in turn made her feel like she was a good mother. I saw through this and confronted her about it. She was in denial over the whole issue and wouldn't balk at the notion of cutting back on her spending. You see this today with many Americans who buy vehicles, televisions, homes, and other things with reckless abandon.

Eventually, it was obvious that a more serious intervention was needed. I gathered some evidence, this time, to support my claims of her errant ways, all the while hoping she would see the proverbial light. This was no easy task, as it took years to chip away at her shield of ignorance. One day, it suddenly dawned on her. She needed to stop all of the excessive spending. Many Americans were awakening to this nightmare and were correcting there ways, at least temporarily.

I followed by telling her something that can be applied of others. You're free to make excessive purchases, but follow this general guideline. Can you afford it? If you have the extra income, after the necessities are taken care of, feel free to treat yourself, but consider the next question first. If you bought this item, would it put you into debt? Think long and hard on this one, and if you do not absolutely need the product, use self-control and wait. By putting thought into the purchase, instead of impulsively buying things, you will save yourself a lot of money.

The average American is shrouded in the guise of wealth with every purchase. Society hasn't frowned on this, as the inner consumer screams out that it's okay to buy. America is still pushing through hard financial times in this economic stagnation. This has made people at least aware of the issues they are facing. The consumerist mentality is still strong, but at least people are showing both awareness and a sense of caution.

Self-image and unnecessary expenditures have left many reeling for a remedy that may never come. Moderate self-control will go a long way. My mother has improved greatly, but she is still guilty of the occasional mishap. If Americans are not proactive in correcting their behavior, this downturn in the economy will only get worse.

Zombies, Velociraptors, Safety, and You

Derek Dowen

Hudson Valley Community College's Public Safety Department has adapted their safety policies to include the ever-impending "Zombie Apocalypse." But could they be overlooking another threat that could very well be upon our doorstep any day? They are, in fact, overlooking the hunting powers of the Velociraptor. But which should HVCC be more worried about; the skilled hunting Velociraptor or the ever-hungry Zombie? To get a good picture, one must compare the two.

Zombies, when compared to Velociraptors, are relatively easy to understand. They were once human creatures that feed on humans, and they require no real food or nutrients. Zombification is caused by a disease that roots itself in the brain. It's spread by any kind of bodily fluid from a zombie, either saliva or blood, ending up in the blood stream of a human. The infection travels through the bloodstream and infects the brain, where it shuts down all bodily systems and turns the human into a human eating zombie. Since this is how zombies come to be, it doesn't take long for one zombie to become ten, or ten to become one hundred. It is also one of the best forms of psychological warfare; it is not easy to watch your husband, mother, wife, brother, uncle, or anyone you are close to turn into a zombie, especially when you know what you must do to ensure the survival of everyone else. With the sheer amount of zombies that may be out there, it seems they would take over fairly quickly. Well, when humans become zombies, they lose a lot of human qualities; they no longer have the ability to think, and their brains can only focus on feeding. Their motor movements are reduced to about a step every few seconds, and they lose the ability to climb or do anything that requires thought or complex movement. They are also very loud; often they can be heard moaning from afar. If you combine that with a zombie's speed, they are pretty easy to avoid. If you are unable to avoid them though, it won't be easy to get away. You basically have three choices: fight, flight, or become zombie chow. If you choose flight, be ready for the distance run; zombies never grow tired, so they will be chasing you long after you have stopped to rest. They also don't require food or nutrients to sustain themselves, as stated earlier, so they could potentially chase you for years, or until they eventually rot away. If you have chosen fight, be ready to fight a few, or maybe more than a few zombies. Since zombies are drawn to noise and light, the sound of other zombies moaning, or the sounds of combat such as gun shots, is likely to bring more zombies into the fight. The most important thing to remember is that zombies do not feel pain, so try as you like to hit them continually in the chest, but the only way to completely stop a zombie is to hit in on the head and destroy the brain.

The name Velociraptor means "Swift Thief." This is an appropriate name from them since they are swift and they will steal your life at any second. Velociraptors are just like most natural creatures on earth; they need food to survive, and we are their food. They also need to mate and birth their young, which come from eggs. They, like zombies, run on two feet; but where a zombie moves slowly, a raptor can reach up to speeds of sixty kilometers per hour for up to fifteen seconds. Their body shapes also differ from zombies to help them run, where a zombie would be the size and shape of whatever human they have infected, the average Velociraptor is about three feet tall and has a long tail threat they use to control their balance. A Velociraptor's main advantage over zombies is its ability to think, even if most of the time it is with animal instinct. They can formulate something of a hunting plan, whereas zombies just attack and swarm. It will also be hard to even know when you are going to be attacked by a Velociraptor; because they are natural born hunters, they tend to be very stealthy and use that stealth to sneak up on prey. When they do sneak up on prey, they will surround it in a triangular pattern so that there would be very little chance of their prey escaping. At this point, there would be no purpose in trying to escape anyway, so fighting would be the only option. Since Velociraptors are living, breathing creatures, it is easier to kill a Velociraptor. The reason for this is that they actually have functioning body parts unlike the zombies. So, if you were to hit the Velociraptor anywhere, it would actually feel it, which also brings the point that they do in fact feel pain. If you were to hurt a Velociraptor enough, it would eventually retreat to tend to its wounds, unlike a zombie, which would continue its way toward you until one of you are no longer moving.

Where Velociraptors and Zombies may be different creatures, they do have similar goals: to make humans their dinner. Obviously, both of these creatures are large threats to the human population, and neither should be underestimated; they are both very formidable opponents and should both be warned against. So, HVCC is seriously overlooking the threat of a Velociraptor takeover, but that doesn't mean they should just trash the Zombie safety plans. Both are equally important to keeping safe the population of healthy and educated college students who are only hungry for more knowledge.

Memories on the Dirty Floor

Brittany DuQuette

There lying on the dirty floor,
Among the dust, dirt, and more.
Glistening as the sunlight flickers,
The air conditioner way off kind of snickers.
No one seems to notice it just lying there.
To everyone, the floor is just bare.
If only they knew the secrets there within.
All the memories buried there within the sin.
The secrets and lies and all of the whys,
All of the easiest hellos and the hardest goodbyes.
A confused girl stumbles through the door,
Among her passing she notices something there on the floor.
There buried among the dust and the dirt galore.
She doesn't think that she can take it anymore.
She holds back here tears; she so badly wants to cry.
All she can manage to whisper is *why*.
She scoops it up within her hands.
She wipes off the extra dust strands.
Her hand slowly withdrawals as she tries to stay calm.
A silver cross is revealed there in her palm.
She rubs the remainder of the dirt,
Using the edge of her shirt.
Something so important should have never gotten pushed from mind,
Maybe it was all to be a sign.
Etched on the back is June 21st 2009.

Once upon a Love Journey

Tracie Endelson

Number one: You were so fun.
You made me smile mile upon mile.
A burst of fresh air, you showed me to care.
Nights of hot tubs, deep conversations
Under stars of mystic creations.
I worshipped your spark that would light up the dark,
But when it was time for me to break free,
You tightened your grip as I began to flee.

Number two: What did I do?
To capture someone genuine and kind as you.
You swept me away
But ultimately, though, I begged you to stay.
A series of triumphs and bumps in the road,
What I saw as a prince, turned into a toad.
I gave you all that I had of my heart
You melted it, froze it, and smashed it apart.

Number three: I gave in hesitantly.
A wizard of exquisite words,
Sent shivers through me like arrows or swords.
You encouraged exploration through many drinks
And a chart to navigate my idled kinks.
You offered a world of pleasure and fantasy.
Who could resist the temptation of ecstasy?
But even you could not plow through
All my barriers that exist; they are not so few.

* * *

Number four: You held the door.
Left flowers on my car; no one did that before,
But you were just as confused as I
And searching for answers I could not supply.

Number five: Are you alive?
In a far away land; will you touch my hand?
Take me in from the tide; will I be your bride?
Won't someone please shake me awake?
So I don't make another mistake.

Wake-Up Call

Maurice Lindsey

Wake-up call! Have you had yours yet? Whoa, let me rewind a little bit. Do you know what a wake-up call is? It's a point in life where a person realizes certain things that are going on around them, yet seemed to go unnoticed until it's too late. Some people never get this call, simply because they may have things more in line or in check as many would say; but as you know everyone is not like that, especially not me. Well I got a real wake-up call at the age of seventeen on Wednesday, January 20, 2010. What exactly happened on this day you may ask? On that very day I found out I was HIV positive. Only the people who have gone through this can describe all the things going through their head or the things they went through after they found out.

An experience this breathtaking is what I call a wake-up call. It was January in Syracuse, New York. For those who don't know much about Syracuse it is Brick City (freezing cold). Yet this winter seemed to be a lovely warm winter, not much snow, or too much wind. The sun was set beautifully in the sky and I was out of school early as usual (one of the great advantages of being an honors student). As I was leaving school, I realized something, I had not been tested since June of 2009. I sat at the bus stop not really thinking much of it; I had only been with the same person for the last year so it didn't really bother me. Thirty minutes later, there I was, two blocks away from the clinic just standing in the middle of the sidewalk trying to decide between getting tested or just going home and forgetting the whole thing.

Of course, being me, I took a walk right into the clinic. I've been in this clinic before, but on this day, nothing seemed the same.

It was dark and there was not one soul in the waiting room. So, I went to the check-in desk and took a number. I didn't look at the number until I sat down and there it was: the number one. I sat there thinking to myself, "Wow, I'm the first person who has been here today." Not even two minutes later a short Dominican man, of no more than five foot three, who weighed well over two hundred pounds, called my number. We walked into the back where the testing rooms were and he introduced himself, stating his full name, where he worked, the reason he worked, and the procedure he was going to perform that morning. With all that overwhelming information at once, I just said my name and the reason I was there.

As he began taking his equipment out I sat there looking around in silence not really thinking much of it because I was sure I was clear of all STDs. Once he was done, he described the type of rapid test I was going to be getting while he was putting on his gloves. Next thing I knew, he poked my index finger with a needle and squeezed it so blood would start to drip out. He took the blood and placed it into the test. He placed a Band-Aid on my finger, and there I was texting on my grey BlackBerry Pearl. Ten minutes went by like a single commercial on television. The exact words that came out his mouth were, "Its positive." Effrin being the caring man he is looked at me and said, "I don't think that was right." So he took it again. The same result came back.

I just sat there without facial expression, speechless as to what I should say next; but I knew from that day on, I had to grow up and grow up fast. Effrin sat there looking at me and asking me, "No tears, no screaming, no reaction? What are you a robot?" I replied, "No, I know what I have to do from here." I gathered my things and walked out the door as if nothing happened. Once I got out the building, the first person I called was my ex-boyfriend. I told him he needed to go get tested as soon as possible and then hung up. The emotions running through my head were crazy. I thought to myself: *How? When? Why? I want to die. What will I say to my mom? How will my next partner take this?* All those questions and so many more were going through my head while I was walking toward my bus to head home.

The bus ride was quiet peaceful and soothing. Once I got home I went straight to my room and went to sleep, because I couldn't think about it anymore. When I woke up, it was six in the evening and I heard my mom cooking, my sister running around, and my brother playing Halo on his PS3. Without getting out of bed, I managed to dig my cell phone out of my bookbag. I had exactly 109 missed calls, 78 text messages, and 49 voicemails; all of which were made within the last two hours. Right then and there, I knew exactly who it was and why they were calling. I erased every message in my inbox without even reading it, deleted every voicemail without even checking them, and returned one of his phone calls.

He picked up the phone and said, "Hello." I sat there in silence trying to gain the strength and find the words to tell him what was going on. Then I took a deep breath and started talking: "Devante, it's been well over two months since the last time I seen you. You're the last person I had sex with, but there is something that doesn't make any sense to me. I got tested today and they said I was HIV positive. From this day on, I will not talk to you; it will seem like I just fell off the face of the earth. I don't know how my status changed from negative to positive within the last seven months and I have only been with you, but all I know is whereever it came from, you gave it to me. I'm not telling you this to play a joke on you or hurt your feelings. You just need to know. Goodbye Devante." Those were not my exact words, but they were similar. As I was saying all of that, I could hear him start to whimper and cry. He sat there speechless, not knowing what to say, and without giving him a chance to speak, I hung up the phone.

After that phone call, he never called back or sent me one message. I knew he was shocked and hurt, but nobody knew the pain I was going through mentally. I ate dinner then went right back to sleep. The next morning, I woke up as usual and went to school as if nothing happened. I refused to let this change me as a person; I was always the happy boy with all the advice. The bell rang and I went to my first block anatomy class. I sat directly behind my friend Meghan, and she showed me her new iPhone. We sat there talking and waiting for class to begin, and then she turned around because Ms. Detore walked into the room yelling the normal, "Phones away, iPods away, gum out, food trash!" As class began, I still was using my phone on my lap. I logged onto my Facebook and I had eight messages in my inbox. I was thinking in my head that was strange because I didn't have any when I left home.

As I began reading the messages all of them said: *Do you have HIV? Are you ok? Who gave it to you? I'm gonna kill you....* Then my phone rang and I bent over as if I was tying my shoe and all I heard were two words: "I'm sorry." I sat back up and continued taking notes and browsing Facebook on my phone. While reading the messages, I sat there wondering how they knew. I hadn't told anyone except one person. Then I had the idea to go to Devante's page. There it stood in his status right next to his picture. "Maurice Lindsey, a senior at Henninger High School, the captain of the cheerleading team is HIV Positive. He is passing it to women and men all around Syracuse, NY. If you cherish your life and your loved ones, you will stay away from this nasty vermin. I hope you die a slow painful death fagget!" The only thing I could do was sit there and cry; tears were falling without me taking one breath. I ran out of class only having two things: my phone and my house keys. I went straight to my best friend's class upstairs, knocked on the door, and asked could she leave the room. She quickly got up from her seat and left the classroom. All she kept saying was, "What's wrong Reese?" I couldn't speak, so I handed her my phone with Devante's page still on my screen. She started crying and swearing up a storm.

Next thing we knew the first block bell rang for students to switch classes. All of our friends stopped and stood around me and Tekquia as we cried and slowly but surely my phone was passed around between all my closest friends. (Still standing in a cluster, all of us were crying.) Then one girl by the name of Joi Jones pulled me aside and said she would handle this. My ladies walked me to my next class and I pulled myself together so I would be able to go to my next class. I couldn't focus in the class at all. An hour and half later, the bell rang for lunch and the entire varsity cheerleading team was outside my classroom waiting for me to come out. Tekquia and Joi were at the head of the pack. Joi said, "We're going to Tully's for lunch." I didn't say anything; I just went along with it. I got in Tekquia's car along with Joi, Jalisa, and Quanira; the car ride there was silent.

When we walked into the restaurant, I saw an entire section just blocked off and it was full of the varsity football team and some of the cheerleader's boyfriends along with an empty table set up just for me and the ladies. We all ordered our food and had a blast eating. At the end of lunch, everyone was paying for their food and Joi paid for my lunch. Next thing I knew, Tekquia, standing four foot eleven stood up on a chair and said, "As you know my boy Reese has a problem, and we're about to solve it. Everyone park along the side of Barry Park next to the soccer fields. Get out of the cars and wait at the playground section, and us ladies will handle the rest." She took her seat. All the boys got up and left; we followed soon after them. I just sat there in silence wondering what was going on, but I was singing in the car.

We pulled up into the park one block away from Devante's house. The girls got out of the car and told me to stay back with the boys. So I followed along with it. Most of the boys I knew some of them I didn't, and even though I was the only gay one, I felt like they all were comfortable being around me. About ten minutes later, the girls walked down to the park with Devante in the midst of the crowd. As they began talking and sitting on the swings all the boys (54 to be exact) got up and said, "Let's go." I did what they said. Within seconds, all I saw were boys holding Devante and beating him senseless. All I did was sit there and watch, not one tear fell from my eye. I sat there and watched this go on for twenty straight minutes until they stopped.

Then we all left, walking to our cars while Devante still conscious had enough strength to dial 911. At this point in time, I felt loved by so many people. They told me that I was one person on this earth that didn't deserve one bit of what happened that day. I was family and always will be family. They told me I was one of the strongest and smartest people they have ever met. The feeling of love was there and I felt it; I could tell that there were people that actually cared about me outside of my real family. During the ride home, my ladies told me they had my back any time.

The main moral behind this story is how people react to a Facebook post that they didn't even know was true. At the end of the day, they knew it was true, but at the spur of the moment, they only knew one thing: that I was disrespected. I can't explain how much this experience has changed my life not only as a person but as a student, a son, a brother, and an overall friend. I realized I've touched people in ways I never knew about. I have helped people on levels I never thought came together for me. This is exactly why I want to become a nurse: because I feel like I have a gift of nurturing and helping that not many people have. To this day I will forever be who I am and have what I have, but I won't let it stop me from living the life that I deserve.

Still, in the back of my mind, I sat there wondering what I was going to tell my family or the next person I would develop feelings for. I couldn't even fathom the number of boys that would turn me down because of the virus, but shockingly, a boy came into my life and is still here now. My boyfriend loves me for everything I am and will be in the future. He said I have skin of steal and the heart of a mother. Nobody can stop my dreams with or without HIV.

Now that's what I call a wake-up call.

Rekindle

Karen Segretto

Suffocating.

Empathy;
Where is empathy when I need it?
Exhausted, yet cannot fall down,
Rest impossible—*angels* refuse it.

Where have those angels been?
All but one seems to have fled;
Omnipresent memories from my time in bliss—
Haunt me now, forcing me to believe in more.

Depleting.

Worn through, like a surviving victim of a stabbing;
Angels, I listened—you told me not to falter,
insisted passions, purpose, must persevere—
Yet with deaf ears in full surround... doom!

Like Maharishi's explanation of Transcendental Meditation,
my Being has reached the bottom of the ocean;
I've touched *down...*
Lower than ever-before imagined.

What goes down must come up... angels do say;
How now?

Survived cancer—remained for my children;
The battle should be over...

yet in some new fashion, the wormhole has reopened;
Dehydration synthesis slowed… DNA repair under pressure.

I *know*
I'm still dying
too fast.
Bleeding!

Love, where did you go?
So you knew little of me then…
When we wed;
now I am unlovable?

Semantics, debate, tangle, love battles…
So this is worth more—
than anything else,
than us?

Abandoned.

My torch is but a dim glow—
Am I supposed to be here?
Treading the path to tend the sick,
Educating *me* and leaving the children to you?

Decrepit scaffold—promised support…
failed footings…crumbled foundation.
Increasing pressures and loads…
These systems collapse.

Redefining.

Again? I suppose 'tis *the only way.*

Firewood

Romey Romano

In the morning light, Alys squinted her eyes as she entered the living room. Out the picture window she saw Ralph walking up the frost covered lawn, gun slung over his shoulder, empty handed. The years were catching up to both of them. Another trip to the grocery store, or another meal of last fall's snap-beans and tomatoes. There were only so many ways she could prepare them, and she felt ill thinking about the mess boiling in a pot.

Once there had been meat on the table and store bought cans in the pantry. Now, rows of Ball jars they'd canned themselves lined one wall of their damp cellar. It was a laborious process that filled their days last fall. Retirement, the "Golden Years" my ass, she thought. Ralphie clumped up the back porch stairs. The mudroom door opened and slammed shut.

Alys walked into the kitchen to greet him. He closed the door to the mudroom and made for the bathroom. He looked at her with watery aged eyes, and reached out with his right hand to cup her cheek. She nestled into his familiar cold hand. He smiled and said, "I'll be right back," and shuffled off to the bathroom.

She'd have breakfast with him. Later today they would work on next year's wood pile. The fuel that warms you up twice. Twice my ass. Cut the tree, saw it up into 18 inch lengths, split it, stack it, and next winter haul it into the house a bit at a time, restack it by the stove, stoke the stove, dig out the ashes, dump 'em into a pile by the garden, and in the spring spread the ashes on the tomato patch. "Twice my ass," she heard herself whisper, and then said, "How about some eggs and snap beans dear?"

The toilet flushed and the sound of running water in the bathroom sink echoed through the little house. "You know how they affect me," he hollered from the bathroom. "First I'll fart up a storm and then I'll shit myself. For Christ's sakes woman, the last time I ate that combination I spent enough time in the crapper to read *War and Peace*."

"Dearest, everything you eat affects you like that, or did you already forget you old coot?" She then set about preparing his second breakfast.

Around eight o'clock, they piled into their '48 Willy's Jeep and drove off into the woods. The homemade trailer, made from the front end of a Ford Model A, bounced along, tethered to the Jeep with a stiff hitch made from an old steel bed frame. Alys had packed a lunch and Ralph had packed his shotgun, just in case he saw some game or a coyote.

They rode along lost in their thoughts, as the birds and chipmunks went along with their spring chores. The road, such as it was, bore the marks of the previous day's trip in the dark rich soil that wasn't quite mud.

They reached the small clearing where they had cut down a number of trees the day before. Crosshatched like pick-up sticks, the trees lay waiting to be limbed and cut into splitting lengths. Alys reached for her bow saw and small axe. Ralph turned from her as he lifted the old chainsaw from the back of the Jeep. He didn't want her to see him wince. She politely turned her back to him, knowing full well the agony that Ralph was going through. This would be the last year that they would be able to harvest their own wood.

"Wood," she thought, "that's something neither of them had seen in their bedroom since Ralph had had his mild stroke." She had her share of problems too; however, the tenderness was still alive. His arms were not as strong as they once were, but Alys still felt comfort snuggling into him every night.

By lunch time they had most of the trees limbed and had started a brush pile. Instead of burning it, they'd leave it. Their excuse being that it would make a good home for the forest critters. The truth of the matter was they were afraid that if a burning brush pile got out of control, they would be powerless to stop it.

They spread their wax-paper–wrapped feast between them on a stump, gave silent thanks, and ate in silence, tossing bits of bread for the animals. For dessert, they shared a slice of apple pie, placing the second piece on a stump. Like Pavlov's dogs, the birds, chipmunks, and squirrels scampered in for the feast. Finished with their meal, they packed up the Jeep and made their way back to the house.

At home, they put away the Jeep and tools. Alys and Ralph couldn't afford the luxury of cable anymore. Instead, they would listen to the radio or read to each other.

Ralph was fidgeting in his Morris chair. "Go take a nap Ralphie." He got out of his chair, kissed her on the cheek, and made his way to the bedroom. Alys heard the bed creak and then picked up a book and started to read where she had left off. As she read, her eyelids became heavier as her breath lengthened toward sleep.

* * *

"Just a few more miles to the folks," Peggy thought. She'd arrive about the time dad would be emerging from the bathroom after his daily hunting expedition. Peggy had picked up fresh-baked cinnamon buns at the store for breakfast.

She parked by the front door and knocked as she opened it. "Mom, Dad, It's Peggy." Alys napped in her chair by the living room picture window, an open book in her lap. Peggy tiptoed to the back of the house and found Dad lying on the queen-sized bed.

She turned and ran to the living room. With a sob, she dropped to her knees by her mother's chair, knowing that both of her parents were dead.

Autumn Girl

Rebecca Vitarelle

Youth runs through her veins.
Warmth flows through her hair and cheeks,
her movements filled with grace.
Her beauty, oh, it chills me.

But this can't last no,
like the summer days long gone,
your fire feels so cold but looks so warm.
So, let's hope all your color lasts until the break of dawn.

Let your ember dance.
Let your true colors show.
Forget about the breeze,
until it covers you in snow.

Winter falls upon you like a storm;
All your colors went away;
they fell, they fell, they fell.
They faded to browns and greys.

They'll all try to smother you.
They'll try to keep you in silence
But you'll spring back, you will.
Your nature is defiance.

All the Fallen Stars

Amanda Smith

I have a dream. Most people do. This miraculous thing about today's generation is that our society has, with confidence and pride, told us to *act* on our dreams. We have the ability to revolutionize the world. Now, when a group of teens sit in their garage and talk about doing something big, they're not fantasizing. They're inventing Google and MySpace. When a bunch of brothers cobble their musical talents together as a band, they become the Jonas Brothers. What teenagers and dreamers have been saying for millennia is dawning on everyone else: Whatever we want is possible. This is a major change from the principles of our forefathers; yet, with a work ethic built on dreams, passion, and entrepreneurship, we feel certain that nothing could go wrong.

But we did go wrong. Visit any business with young employees, and you will witness the problem. My generation comes to work late and gives a mediocre performance. We complain endlessly about our "stupid bosses." We text, surf the web, and chat loudly with coworkers rather than look for ways to improve the job or assist a confused customer. It's embarrassing to watch.

Not all young adults are like this, not by a long shot. Some work hard and do well. But often these employees are ostracized. Their coworkers shrug when the job gets difficult, because they know the hard-worker will deal with it.

This slacker attitude pervades everything my generation attempts—from school, to relationships, to daily life. We struggle and become frustrated, feeling as if we deserve more. My generation has the freedom to develop dreams and follow them through, but we have forgotten that following our dreams is *hard*.

We feel like we deserve easy. If it's not, we shrug and give up. How did this happen? What have we lost? When I ask myself this, I think of my father.

My father is one of a dying breed of men. He retained a work ethic from times before, when men were self-reliant, problem solvers, breadwinners. Parents gave up their personal dreams and desires so that their children could do great things. Men were strong. Women were wise. There was an unspoken but clear understanding that if there wasn't a sacrifice, you weren't doing enough; you failed somewhere. Happiness came if you worked for it. If you weren't happy, you weren't working hard enough.

All his life, my dad has strived after this ideal. I watched him spend hours lying on a sheet of cardboard with his hands stuffed up in the guts of a helpless car, refusing to let it die without a fight—because a man solved his own problems. We had a garden that was larger than our house; one year in a drought, my dad fabricated a network of scrap pipes that pumped water from our brook, and he kept that garden alive. His work ethic is incredible. But our family struggled, as many families do. To my dad, that meant he needed to do more—work harder, be better.

I came to him with my dream once. I wanted to publish a novel, and if my father said I could, then it was fact. But instead, he explained that expecting I could publish a novel was like expecting I could become a rock star. "People try their whole lives to *finish* a novel," he said, "let alone publish it." My dream just wasn't going to happen. If I couldn't see that, I was being naive. My dad was proud of me, but he thought I wasn't facing the truth. In his generation, this was the worst sin you could commit.

My dad crushed me as no one else could have. It hurt that he couldn't set his values aside, not even to say that he believed in me. My father's generation simply cannot deny what they see as facts.

They cannot accept any other way of living other than by hard work, self-sacrifice, and maintaining a do-what-must-be-done attitude.

But the teens of my generation are on the opposite end of the pendulum. Our ethic centers on the individual—what *I* want, what makes *me* happy, how *I* can succeed. We give up the moment it gets hard. The sad part is, half the kids I know are without a life plan, a dream. They've never been challenged to find one. They don't know themselves, and so, they feel lost.

Our parents and grandparents have something to offer. We should value hard work as a chance to prove ourselves. We should care about education, because it gives us the tools to follow our dreams. We should learn to seek out challenges, because without them, we can't learn about our weaknesses or how to overcome them. And society should change its mantra to recognize that having a dream does not mean we deserve its fulfillment.

If we could learn one thing from our grandparents, it would be this: We only deserve the dreams that we fight for.

Just to You I Say

Carol Walkley

I don't really
care that you
left the wheelbarrow in the rain,
chased the cat to the top of the jamcloset,
or ate the plums in the icebox.

Water dries,
cats can climb,
and sweet, cold plums
taste better at night.

There is nothing
to forgive.
Yet so much
depends on the asking.

"Still I Rise," Response

Christina Duerr

The poem I chose to write about is "Still I Rise" by Maya Angelou. The first time I read this poem, it caused goose bumps to run down the length of my arms. It's a powerful display of the inner strength possible even in the face of adversity. At the end of the poem, during the last three lines, I remember actually feeling the words of the poem. I sat there having a physical reaction to "I rise, I rise, I rise," as if my blood pressure knew the strong meaning of the words. I immediately felt a connection to this poem. There have been a few times in my life when I have been called to rise above the obstacles that lie in my path. Sometimes it's been a conscious decision, and sometimes it's been an inherent strength that for the life of me, I don't know where it comes from. I felt compelled to write about this poem because the speaker talks of strength, courage, and such pure self-knowledge of herself that I found it awe-inspiring. I want that. It's what I'm working toward.

I didn't have a very good beginning. I was born in 1972 to a sixteen year old who gave birth to me on a kitchen table with the help of a midwife. Her mother had died when she was very young, and her father wasn't really around, so she basically raised herself. She was a bartender and had random friends watch me while she worked. Surprisingly, she managed to keep me for a few years until the fateful day that I was taken away by the police. It turns out that I was growing up in a house that was a known drug spot. There was a raid on the house, and while the house was being searched, I was found in a closet, dirty and underfed. Thank God I have no memory of this event or the time preceding it, but I'm sure that, even as a small child, I was given the unspoken message that I wasn't important. After being removed from the home, I was placed in foster care where I remained until the age of seven, when I was adopted by a nice couple with two older girls. It was a nice situation, but I always felt different from them, and when I look back, I think I was treated a little differently too.

I would have random visits with my mom throughout the years, but more often than not, she wasn't around and I was getting used to it. There were many times I would be left waiting for her to arrive, and she just wouldn't show up. I would be heartbroken. By the age of twelve, she disappeared completely. She was nowhere to be found. I remember sending her a letter, and a few weeks later, I received that same letter back with "return to sender" stamped in red on the front of the envelope. I still remember that day. She didn't want me. Twenty-five years later, and it's still so vivid. I think it was a defining moment in my life. All the nightmares made sense now; my childhood was plagued with recurring nightmares of being abandoned or not being able to find my way home or just plain being chased by people trying to kill me. I felt alone and I only had myself to depend on. Oh how I cried that night. When the speaker talks of "shoulders falling down like teardrops, weakened by my soulful cries," I am reminded of just how much I cried that night. The fear, the loss was more than my young mind could bear. I was changed that night. I knew I would be different than her.

I believe it is only through pain that one truly grows. All of my major life lessons stemmed from really painful times in my life. Actually, it feels like most of my life has been pretty painful so far. I've battled depression, addiction, and self-hatred just to name a few. Often when I think I've got one under control, another pops up in its place. Challenges, I like to now call them. I've taken their power away; no longer do they control my life.

I think it was about four years ago that my life had begun to change. I was no longer relying on alcohol and drugs to make it through the day. I was in a program of recovery that was transforming my life for the better. I was only five months sober when I found out I was having my daughter Sophia. What a surprise it was, since I wasn't even sure I wanted to have children. I had never really thought about it. But here I was, about to be a mommy. I was petrified that I wouldn't know. I mean what example had I had?

Three years ago, I gave birth to my daughter Sophia. Oh how she is loved. She was born six weeks early, which was a bit of a scare since she only weighed four and a half pounds. But have no fear, she is as healthy as can be, and I cherish every moment I spend with her. Never could I imagine putting her in a closet or denying her food. I couldn't dream of it.

The cycle of abuse has been broken. My daughter will not have the same feelings that I had as a child growing up. She knows that she is loved. She doesn't question that she will be provided for, and that makes me feel good. The speaker of the poem says, "Into a daybreak that's wondrously clear, I rise." That is how I feel: My eyes have been opened. I have been given the grace of a second chance. No longer am I a victim, but a survivor, and that is why I relate to this poem so much. Every day I make a choice to "rise" in spite of many things that long to bring me down. Just like the speaker, I am a fighter too.

Reflect

Candice Knibbs

Pink and orange hangs in the air,
As the Great Wolf releases his catch.
Gold shines through the dangling
Ice crystals about the window,
Dulling the light, and yet
Magnifying.
As the sun rises higher
The skies are blanketed white,
Mirroring the ground.
Flittered,
Only a soft glow remains.
A sky of gentle
White.
An earth of tender
White.
Sky and
Earth
Merge to one.
All
A looking-glass.